Playhouses, Gazebos, & Sheds

Playhouses, Gazebos, & Sheds

Percy W. Blandford

TAB TAB BOOKS
Blue Ridge Summit, PA

FIRST EDITION
SECOND PRINTING

Library of Congress Cataloging-in-Publication Data

Blandford, Percy W.
    Playhouses, gazebos & sheds / by Percy W. Blandford.
        p.   cm.
    Includes index.
    ISBN 0-8306-3604-8
    1. Playhouses, Children's—Design and construction—Amateurs'
manuals.   2. Pavilions—Design and construction—Amateurs' manuals.
3. Outbuildings—Design and construction—Amateurs' manuals.
I. Title.   II. Title: Playhouses, gazebos, and sheds.
TH4967.B57   1992
690'.89—dc20   91-34061
                                                          CIP

TAB Books offers software for sale. For information and a catalog, please contact
TAB Software Department, Blue Ridge Summit, PA 17294-0850.

Acquisitions Editor: Kimberly Tabor
Book Editor: April D. Nolan
Director of Production: Katherine G. Brown
Cover Design: Paul Saberin, Chambersburg, PA
Cover Illustration: Denny Bond, East Petersburg, PA   HT3

Contents

Introduction

This book covers the making of a great variety of small buildings, mainly from wood. They are not homes to live in, but they are the places you might like to have in your yard or garden, at a weekend retreat, on a sport or recreation field, or anywhere that storage facilities or shelter would be needed.

The following pages contain a selection of the instructions and projects in *Small Buildings* (TAB 3144), together with some more new projects, resulting in a varied collection of detailed instructions for small wooden building construction. You should be able to find a design that will suit your needs as it is or can be adapted, accompanied by the full instructions you require.

The buildings range in size from little more than lockers to places to house vehicles, equipment, or stock. Perhaps your first reaction is that anything so big would make a daunting project. It need not be so. You will be handling large pieces of wood and will need space to work, but the actual construction processes are generally simpler than making furniture or toys. You will make more use of hammer and nails. Nearly all joints are simpler. Extreme precision is less important.

If you have done simple woodwork around the home, made basic furniture items, or amused the children with homemade toys, you have the skill to make any building described in this book. If you have a few basic hand tools, you can make almost any of the buildings included in these pages. If you are already a skilled carpenter or cabinetmaker and have a well-equipped shop, that is an obvious advantage, but the beginner with the necessary hand tools can get the same results; it will just take a little longer. Size might make parts heavier, but cutting a joint on wood 15 feet long is no more difficult than it is on a piece 2 feet long.

You might be worried that a building you make might be out of shape and that your mistake will be obvious to anyone who sees it. It is a fact that your approach to marking and setting out must be different. You can use squares and rules on individual pieces of wood, but they are of little use when you need to set out a square of 20 feet or so. Actually, the techniques for squaring a building in all directions are simple and interesting, as you will discover in later pages.

Making and erecting small buildings differ mainly from other branches of woodworking in being less compact. You need to plan ahead the steps in assembly and erection. You might need help handling some of the subassemblies. Do all you can to individual pieces before building them into an assembly—it is usually easier to make a cut or drill a hole on the bench. All of the processes involve the woodwork you know already, but on a larger scale.

Making a small wooden building is a very satisfying form of carpentry. At the end of the work, your product is certainly large enough for others to see. You can look at it and say , "I made that," and others will look at it and ask where you got such a marvelous building!

With individual work you can fit a building to suit needs or a particular space or situation. You can place doors and windows where they suit needs best. The building will be much better than a mass-produced building that has to be accepted as a set design. If you make one or more buildings for your own use and this sort of woodworking appeals to you, neighbors might ask you to make small buildings for them. If you wish, you could find yourself fully occupied in a custom-building small business.

In my many woodworking activities, I have found making small buildings among the most satisfying. I built my own workshop many years ago. It still encourages me to tackle work in it to a high standard, knowing that it is not only well built, but that I planned its size, shape, and arrangement of windows and doors to make the best possible use of the situation. No factory-produced sectional building could compete.

I hope you will find buildings described in the following pages that will show you the work is well within your scope. In a short time you will have the satisfaction of looking at and using your own shed, shop, playhouse, barn, or whatever appeals to you.

Note: Sizes on drawings and in materials lists are nearly all in inches. A few longer measurements are in feet and inches. Widths and thicknesses quoted are nominal, but lengths are mostly a little full. If you are doubtful about the meaning of any building term, the glossary should help you.

1

Preparations

Even the smallest building is probably bigger than the majority of woodworking projects you make, and its size introduces a few special considerations. Instead of doing layout and squaring assemblies on the bench, you are faced with floor areas and structures larger than your normal equipment can span. It would be unwise, for instance, to use a 12-inch square and extend its line to 6 feet, as the possible error at the limit could be more than would be acceptable. Instead, it is better to use geometric methods, preferably to a size larger than the final result has to be so you can avoid possible errors.

It should be safe to assume that the corners of a sheet of 4-×-8-foot plywood are square, so within the limits of that size, you can use a sheet of plywood for marking and checking corners. It might be worthwhile to make a 45-degree triangle by cutting from the corner of a sheet equal lengths along each side. You could use the edge of a sheet of plywood as a straightedge, but it would be better to find your straightest piece of wood of greater length than that, and use it as a straightedge. You can check its straightness by drawing a line against it on a flat surface, then turning it over to see if the line matches (FIG. 1-1A).

If you want to mark long lines, it is better to use a chalk line. Rub a piece of fine line (crochet cotton is suitable) with chalk, without jerking it so the chalk is shaken off. Stretch the line, and have an assistant hold one end down, or use an awl (FIG. 1-1B). Reach as far along as you can, then lift the line a few inches and let it go, to deposit a fine line of chalk on the floor (FIG. 1-1C). If the length is so great that you cannot reach near the middle of the line, get someone else to "snap" the line at its center.

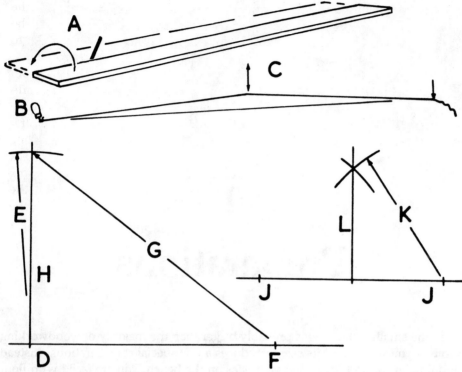

Fig. 1-1. Check straightness by turning a board over. Striking a cord (B) will produce a long line. Make right angles by measuring (D,E,F,G,H) or drawing arcs (J,K,L).

If you need to get a large corner square, as you would for a foundation or floor, draw a baseline longer than you will need. Mark on it where the square line is to come (FIG. 1-1D). Now use the geometric property of right-angled triangles (90 degrees) with sides 3:4:5 proportionally. The right angle is between the two shorter sides.

Choose sizes for the sides of the triangle that will result in the square line you draw being at least as long as the final size you need. Suppose you need 12 feet. If that is the "3" side of the triangle, the unit to use is 4 feet, making the triangle sides 12 feet, 16 feet, and 20 feet. Use a steel tape measure or other convenient means of measuring to draw a short arc from the point on the baseline at 12 feet radius (FIG. 1-1E). The arc should swing over what obviously will be the position of the square line. From the point, measure 16 feet along the baseline (FIG. 1-1F). From that point, measure 20 feet to a position on the arc (FIG. 1-1G). From the starting point, draw a line through the mark on the arc with a chalk line or a long straightedge (FIG. 1-1H). This line will be square to the baseline. Measure other lines parallel to it or the baseline.

If you want to erect a line square to the baseline away from a corner, you can measure equal distances on each side of where it is to be (FIG. 1-1J), then swing arcs from these points (FIG. 1-1K). Draw your square line through the point on the baseline and the crossing of the arcs (FIG. 1-1L). Arrange sizes so the radii of the arcs come at about 45 degrees to the baseline to get a crossing high enough to give a length of square line as big as you need.

The best way to check the squareness of anything you assemble, when opposite sides are the same length, is to compare diagonal measurements. In an ordinary rectangular frame, measure corner to corner (FIG. 1-2A) and adjust the frame until these lengths are the same. You do not have to use the extreme corners. If it is more convenient, take other points that should be square, or measure along the sides from the corners (FIG. 1-2B). You can use the same technique to check the symmetry of anything that is not square (FIG. 1-2C). As assembly of a building progresses, you can compare diagonal or other measurements that should be the same. As the building takes a cubic form, you can compare the distance from the top corner of one side with the bottom corner of another.

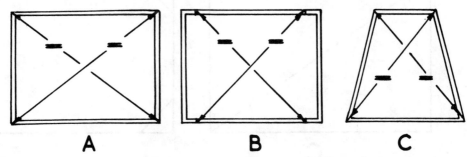

A   **B**   **C**

Fig. 1-2. To check squareness and symmetry, compare diagonal measurements.

Rigidity of Small Buildings

It is useless to try to achieve squareness if what you make is so poorly designed or made that it goes out of shape. The ability to hold a shape depends mainly on triangulation. If you join four pieces loosely at the corners and one corner is pushed, the frame will go out of shape (FIG. 1-3A). If you make a three-piece frame (FIG. 1-3B), nothing can push it out of shape. Put a diagonal piece across the four-sided frame, and you have two triangles (FIG. 1-3C). Providing no parts bend, this framework will hold its shape. Smaller triangles might be sufficient (FIG. 1-3D). If you cover a framework with plywood, you have thoroughly triangulated it, and its shape will hold, but if you nail boards across, movement is still possible and it is advisable to add one or more struts to provide triangulation.

In a roof truss, you have the rigidity of a triangle, whether the tie-in is at the eave's level or higher (FIG. 1-3E) to provide head room. Any other framing in a roof truss is there to provide stiffness, but it also contributes to rigidity.

In a large roof, you support the covering on lengthwise purlins attached to the rafters. The assembly is comparable to a squared framework. Some stiffness

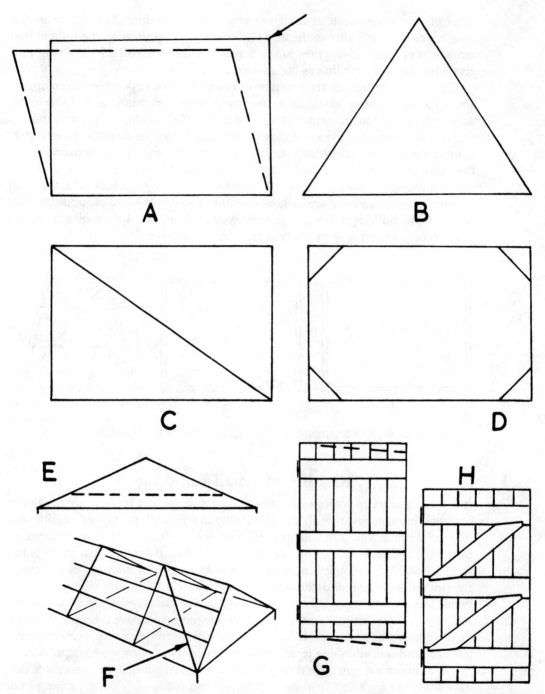

Fig. 1-3. *A four-sided assembly might push out of shape (A). A three-sided figure will not push out of shape (B). Stiffen four-sided frames by triangulating them (C,D,E,F). To prevent a door from sagging, use diagonal braces (G,H).*

comes from the building below, but triangulating the roof will relieve that of the excessive load. If the roof covering is made up of large sheets of stiff plywood rigidly fixed down, that will be sufficient. On the other hand, if the covering is made of many sheets of corrugated metal, plastic, or something similar, movement is possible and diagonal wind bracing (FIG. 1-3F) might be advisable.

Triangulation also might be necessary in smaller assemblies, such as doors. If you make a door with several upright boards and ledgers nailed across (FIG. 1-3G), the door will soon sag. To prevent this sagging, add braces (FIG. 1-3H), preferably notched into the ledgers. If the door tries to sag, the compression loads on the braces stop it.

If you are making the side of a shed or something similar, consider all the parts that are being built in, such as windows and doors or anything that will be inside and attached. If there will not be an absolutely rigid skin and the lines are all parallel in two directions, add some diagonal struts to keep the assembly in shape. Long struts are most effective, but smaller, diagonal braces can give considerable stiffness.

Foundations of Small Buildings

Rarely do you erect a building directly on the ground. Usually you have to prepare a base on which it stands and to support it. You might want to use a sectional building temporarily—such as with a shed used for garden tools during the summer months only, or another building you plan to use only briefly and then move it to another position. A dirt floor might be acceptable in this case, but you still must level it. Even a temporary building that is obviously not level looks wrong to you and all other observers. If you erect walls out of true, you will have difficulty fitting the roof.

Compacted soil might take the weight of a small building, but you must ram it or roll it hard before you put a building on it. If soil settles under the weight of a wall, you might have difficulty lifting and supporting it to make it level.

Even if you are satisfied with a dirt floor, it is usually better to arrange more solid supports under the walls. You could dig out a shallow trench and fill it with sand and small stones rammed tightly together (FIG. 1-4A). Better solutions would be to use concrete for the top few inches (FIG. 1-4B) or to embed anchor bolts as shown in FIG. 1-4C. With stones only, you will have to drive spikes through them into the ground.

Another alternative is to use bricks or concrete blocks. It might be satisfactory to put them in line (FIG. 1-4D), but you can spread the load better if you place them crosswise (FIG. 1-4E).

Wood as a foundation material can rot. Some woods have a good resistance to rot, and woods soaked in preservative will certainly have a reasonable life. However, keep in mind that merely painting preservative on your wood does not achieve much penetration and would have little effect. Old railroad ties are a very good source because they are saturated with preservative and should be immune to rot.

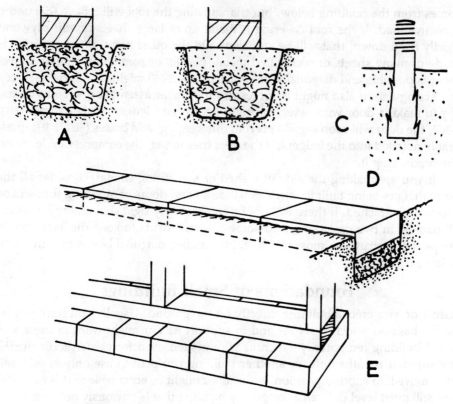

Fig. 1-4. A wooden building needs firm foundations.

The most common foundations for wooden buildings consist of an all-over concrete pad. You can extend it outside to form a path or patio; you also can use it as the floor of the building if that will suit its use.

A floor made of something other than dirt is also a good seal against moisture and rodents. The thickness and the way you form the foundation will depend on the state of the ground. On a hard soil, you could cover a few inches of rammed, small stones with 3 inches of concrete, but if the soil is loose and sandy, you would need to increase both thicknesses.

Most ground is not as level as you would wish. If you want to put the building on the side of a hill, the slope is obvious. You might have to make a foundation pad partly into the slope at the back and build it up at the front.

On apparently level ground you might find a few inches difference in the length of the building, and you must allow for that. You must consider the circumstances and decide if you want one end above the surrounding ground or if you should go deeper at the other end. A compromise might be more appropriate. This decision applies whether you are putting down foundations under the walls only or laying an over-all pad.

For leveling, use the longest possible level, but supplement it with a long, straight board, preferably to span the whole foundation diagonally. It would be unwise to use the level alone to check a distance much greater than its own length.

Start with one side. If you will be putting down blocks, drive in several pegs as guides so their tops are level (FIG. 1-5A). You can use this procedure for a concrete foundation, or you might put down the shuttering strip, making sure its top is level with what will be the top surface of the concrete (FIG. 1-5B). Use pegs on both sides of the strip and pack it so it cannot move once you have it level and straight.

Next, work square to the first side, setting out the angle as described earlier. Level the pegs or shuttering in the same way. As a final check on that side, put your leveling strip across diagonally (FIG.1-5C). If your leveling strip does not show a true level, test the other ways again—you do not want a twist in the foundation.

Level the remaining two sides in the same way. Mark them parallel to the first sides. Level each in the same way as the first side (FIG. 1-5D). Also, check both diagonals. If you will be putting down a complete pad of concrete, put a few pegs in so that their tops are level with the shuttering in the body of the base (FIG. 1-5E). Use them as guides to leveling or laying the stones over which you will put the concrete. Pull them out as you lay the concrete.

If you are only laying concrete under the walls, put in the inner shuttering (FIG. 1-5F), making sure it is level as you progress. If you are putting down bricks, blocks, railroad ties, or other sectional-foundation material, lay it with the pegs as guides, but check it frequently with your level. You can do little to correct unlevel surfaces once the mixture has set.

This is not a book on concrete work, so you should always follow the supplier's recommendations. If your foundation is in a position where you can have ready-mixed concrete delivered and shot, that might be the best way of preparing a foundation. You probably will settle for more than adequate thickness. If you mix the concrete yourself, do not be tempted to lay only a thin layer to save money or time. Have a good, consolidated base of sand and stones, with about 3 inches of concrete, even if the only weight on it will be light storage and standing people. For storage of yard machinery or a car, use an increased thickness of concrete. Thin concrete might crack, even if you do not load it heavily.

An alternative to laying concrete as a one-piece foundation, especially where it also will be the floor, is to put down precast concrete slabs. You can buy them plain or with decorated or stone-like surfaces. You can spread slabs about 24 inches square over a large area quickly. Bed them in sand and small stones, making sure they are level as you progress. They need not have anything between them, although you can seal spaces with concrete. If you seal the spaces with concrete, make sure it is more than 1/2 inch thick; very thin concrete mortar tends to crack and break away. Open spaces filled with soil are appropriate to the floors of summerhouses or sun lounges, where you might consider grass or small plants taking root there attractive.

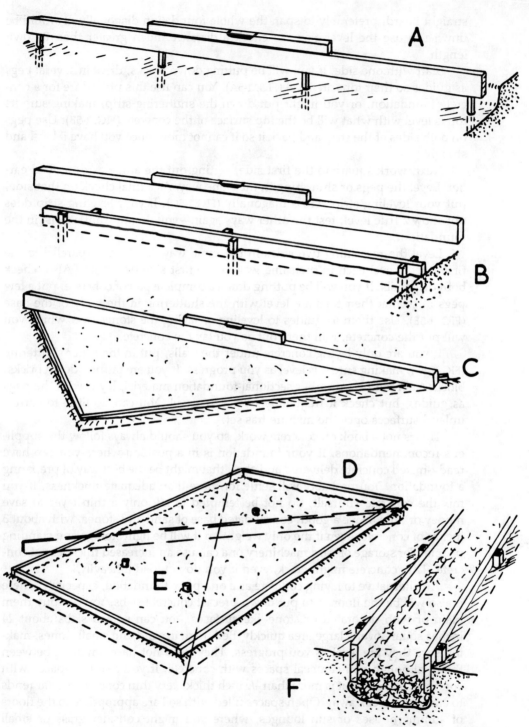

Fig. 1-5. *Check foundation levels in all directions.*

Floors of Small Buildings

In many buildings, the floor and the foundation will be the same thing. A concrete floor is acceptable for many purposes. If you will be driving a car or a tractor over it or if there is a risk of spilling oil or water on it, concrete should be the choice. If it is a workshop or other building where you will spend some time and might drop tools or equipment, a wooden floor is more comfortable and less liable to damage dropped tools. If it is a building for year-round use, a wooden floor gives a more equitable temperature underfoot. You can coat concrete with rubberized or plastic sealants that might give you 1/4 inch of insulation and a more comfortable surface, but these are not as satisfactory as wood for long-term standing.

The usual wooden floor in a small building might be very similar to the floors in many houses, with boards laid over joists (FIG. 1-6A). Sections of wood and

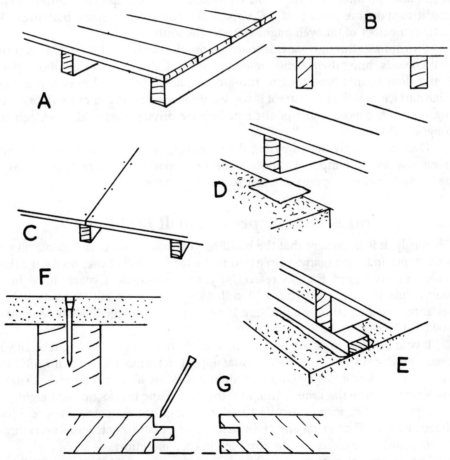

Fig. 1-6. A floor may be boards or particleboard on joists (A,B,C). Insulate wood from concrete (D,E). Conceal nails (F,G).

spacing of the wood will depend on the size of the floor and the amount of support needed. As a guide, you can support boards which are $7/8$ inch thick on 2-×-4-inch joists at 15-inch centers in an average small building (FIG. 1-6B). In a very small building, the joists need only be 3 inches deep. Particleboard, at least $3/4$ inch thick, makes a good alternative to parallel boards. With joints on joists, you have the minimum of gaps (FIG. 1-6C).

Avoid joists or other wood resting directly on concrete, brick, or stone. If you are supporting the ends of joists at wall foundations, insulate them from moisture (FIG. 1-6D). This insulation might be material sold for damp-proofing or for roof covering, or just pieces of plastic sheeting. If you intend to support the length of the joists by the concrete foundation, put strips of plastic under them or cover the whole concrete surface with plastic sheeting. It might be better to raise the wooden floor above the foundations, especially if the concrete is not level in the main area. Even if the wooden floor starts apparently level, eventually it might take the uneven shape of the concrete below. A strip over damp-proofing might support the joists (FIG. 1-6E) above the concrete. In some buildings, the bottom member of the wall might support the joists.

Punch nails through particleboard below the surface (FIG. 1-6F). If you use plain boards, bring them tightly together and sink their nails below the surface. Better floor boards have tongue-and-groove joints. They will maintain a more even surface, which is important if you want to lay carpeting or other floor covering. You can conceal most of their nailing by driving diagonally through the tongues (FIG. 1-6G).

One surprisingly hard-wearing floor covering is hardboard. In damp conditions, use the oil-tempered variety. Fasten it down with plenty of fine pins or nails. An initial wax spray or polish should seal it for life.

Sizes and Shapes of Small Buildings

Obviously, it is important that the building you make can accommodate all you want to put in it. Too many people find that after a period of use, they wish their building were bigger. For this reason, if you have sufficient space, it might be worthwhile to plan sizes that will suit more than your initial needs. If, for instance, you are planning a building 10 feet long, it costs relatively little more to make it 12 feet long.

If your building is purely utilitarian, a functional appearance might be all you need, but if you want to consider visual appeal, remember that having all three main sizes different has a better look than if they are almost the same. Usually, the length is more than the width, and the roof shape breaks up the height.

Plywood and many manufactured building boards come in 4-×-8-foot sheets. If you will be using any of these materials, plan sizes to suit them whole, or cut in only one direction, for economy in cost and effort.

The ground plan of most buildings is rectangular, and there is usually no advantage in departing from this shape. The building is simple to make, and there are no problems with fitting any type of roof. Tapering the plan is unwise because you must then adapt the roof, either by sloping its ridge or sloping the eaves—neither of which looks right.

An L shape is possible, maybe to provide a porch for the door, to keep the main floor clear, or to reduce drafts (FIG. 1-7A). For a pergola or summerhouse, you could have an *octagon* shape (FIG. 1-7B) or a *hexagon* shape (FIG. 1-7C). The former is slightly simpler at roof level because you are basically working with a square with its corners cut off.

You need at least 75 inches of clearance for comfortable head room. A storage shed where you do not expect to spend much time inside might have less, or you might provide standing head room over only part of the area. With a *ridge roof*, you can provide this area by using a central end door (FIG. 1-7D). With a *sloping roof*, you might have the door at the higher side of the building (FIG. 1-7E). If you plan to fill the lower parts with shelves or other storage, the limited height might not matter.

A variety of roofs are possible. The simplest roof is a *flat roof* (FIG. 1-7F). This roof might be adequate for some purposes, but in the long term, it can be more troublesome than any other roof. If it is made absolutely flat, it might sag at the center. A slight slope from one side to the other or from the center outwards is advisable.

Next is the sloping, or *lean-to*, roof (FIG. 1-7G). On a fairly narrow building, this roof might be all you need. A moderate slope will shed rainwater, but if you want it to clear heavy snow, the slope must be greater, and that might affect accommodation and appearance.

A *ridge roof with vertical gables* is most popular (FIG. 1-7H), and for many structures, this is all you need. To most people, it looks right and it does all a roof should do. Inside there is good head room and, if the walls are over 72 inches high, you might arrange storage capacity in the roof area. A change to a *hip roof* reduces wind resistance (FIG. 1-7J). On a building of moderate size, you can make this change at one or both ends to improve appearance.

A *double-slope* roof (FIG. 1-7K) has a typical American barn appearance. More work is involved in making it, but the head room is increased over the central area. If you make a hexagonal building, you must cut some complicated rafter angles. In effect, you are making a hip roof all around (FIG. 1-7L).

Curved roofs are possible (FIG. 1-7M), but they are generally better for larger buildings. They are considerably more work unless you use curved, corrugated metal or plastic sheeting, which is almost self-supporting.

Windows in Small Buildings

With the smallest storage building, you might get sufficient light inside when you open the door, but nearly all other buildings should have windows. Even with a windowless, small, box-like structure, it might be worthwhile to arrange a flap or shutter in a wall or opposite the door, for more light or possibly for passing things through.

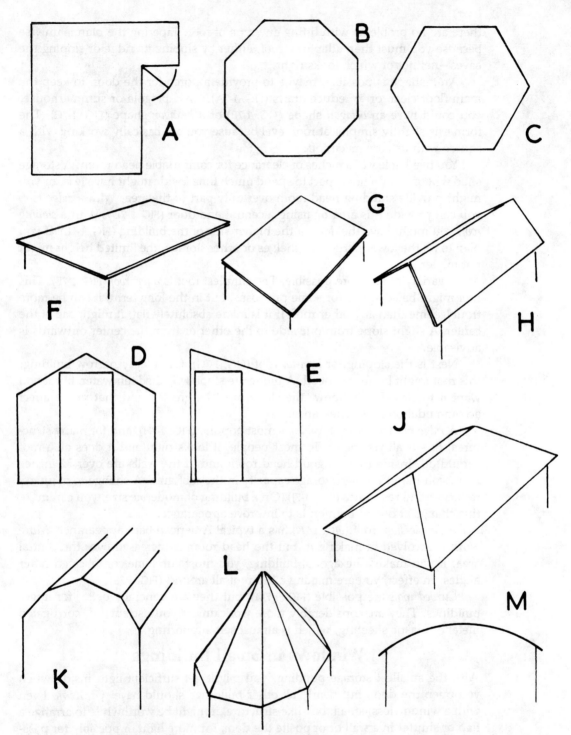

Fig. 1-7. You can plan buildings in many shapes and with different roofs.

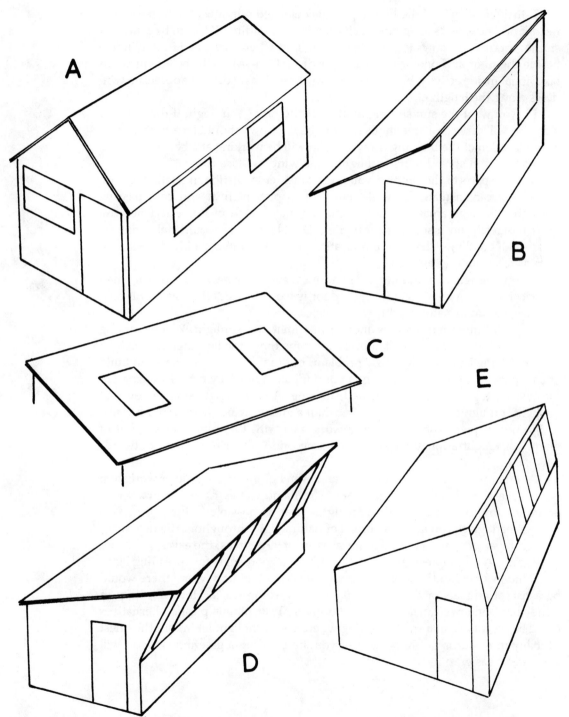

Fig. 1-8. Arrange in walls (A,B) or roof (C). Sloping windows give different types of illumination.

Consider the use of the building. A few isolated windows might be all you need if no one expects to spend much time in the building. If it is to be a shop or studio, arrange windows to provide natural light where you need it. A window beside the door and one or more at the sides (FIG. 1-8A) might be adequate for occasional inside activity, but for lengthy work sessions, you will appreciate windows along the length of a side (FIG. 1-8B).

Do you want the sun shining in most of the time? You might if the window side also will serve as a greenhouse. If so, the windows should face south, so far as the location of the building allows. If you will be working at a bench, you will get a more even spread of natural light if the windows face north.

In some parts of the country, you must consider insulation in relation to windows. You can insulate the walls and roof to prevent heat and cold passing through, but large areas of glass might eliminate much of this effect because glass has really no insulating properties. Double glazing would help, but for most small buildings, that is a complication you will want to avoid. It is better to have as few windows as possible.

If you arrange the windows to open, make sure they have a good seal when you close them. A small window in a door is worth considering, as it will help with the spread of natural light.

Daylight through the roof is another possibility for sunlight. When working inside, overhead lighting is often more welcome than side lighting(FIG. 1-8C).

Preventing leakage might be a problem, but roof lights are available to build in as a package. Making your own is not difficult. You easily can fit transparent plastic sheeting into metal-corrugated sheeting. A surprisingly small amount of daylight through the roof will be better than a greater window area in the walls.

To obtain plenty of lighting in a work area with the minimum amount of glare, you might arrange windows all along one wall so they slope outwards (FIG. 1-8D).

Another way to provide maximum and even lighting in a studio or workshop is to make a *north-light roof* (FIG. 1-8E). The name comes from the practice of arranging the roof with the glass facing as near as possible to the north. This arrangement gives you an even spread of natural light throughout the day, without much risk of glare. If the ridge surfaces are at 90 degrees, the eaves angles are 30 degrees and 60 degrees, bringing the glass at a good angle for spreading light.

Windows only in the roof are a good idea for a building where there would be a risk of animals or vandals breaking glass in the walls. However, keep in mind that windows do not have to be glass. Transparent plastic alternatives could be acceptable in a small building where you want light let in, but the finest visibility in or out is not important. If you are building a greenhouse, you will find plastic easier to use.

2

Building Materials

You can use several types of materials to make small buildings. Brick or stone provide the most substantial structures, but you also can make buildings completely of metal, or ones with wooden frames and metal covering. Some plastic materials are suitable for cladding and roofing over wood or metal supports. Using manufactured boards with a wooden base in parts of a building is also acceptable. Nonetheless, most small buildings are made of wood throughout, or with only small amounts of other materials.

This book is for the woodworker who wants to make one or more small buildings and prefers to use the material he knows. Most of the work is quite straightforward and does not have the complications associated with making good furniture or with similar, better-quality woodworking. Obviously, skill is worth having, but you can do much of the work successfully with minimal skill simply by working carefully.

If you have a comprehensive tool kit, you will certainly find uses for it, but it is possible to make many buildings with very few tools, particularly if you get all the wood sawed and planed to size from a lumberyard.

You can use hand or power tools. The main advantages of using power tools are that they can speed up some operations, and they might allow you to gain accuracy, particularly when you prepare parts in the workshop. Once on the site, though, you are more likely to reach for a handsaw or a plane, and you will make much use of a hammer, for which there is no satisfactory power alternative.

The most useful power tool is an electric drill. A router with a few plain cutters will speed up the making of joints. If you have a portable power saw, you will use it, but you can cut most wood for your building easily with a handsaw.

Materials

You can use almost any wood for a small building. Much will depend on what is available in your area. Some woods are more durable than others, but preservatives on the less-durable woods will give them a long life. In general, there is no need to use hardwood. Most hardwoods are harder to work with than softwoods, and they are unnecessarily heavy. Most are also considerably more expensive than softwoods. Some very resinous woods have a good resistance to rot, and you can even use a few of these without treatment on the outside. Consequently, such woods weather to a pleasant color that might blend in well with the surroundings. Normally, though, you should paint or treat most small wooden buildings so they are protected from the effects of sun and rain.

Any of the common softwoods are acceptable choices for your wooden buildings. Wood with a few small knots should work satisfactorily, but for the structural parts, try to get wood with reasonably straight grain and few knots. If a knot is black around its outside, it is loose and will not contribute to strength, even if it does not fall out. Of course, a knot that falls out of cladding or siding would be a nuisance. Knots without black rims are less trouble.

For many parts of most small buildings you can use sawed wood, but where it will show, it is better to use planed wood. Planing at a mill will reduce sizes by about 1/4 inch, and you must allow for that. For instance, 2-×-4-inch wood planed all around actually will be about $1^3/4 \times 3^3/4$ inches. If the structure will be hidden between the outside covering and an inner lining, you could use sawed wood and get the benefit of extra strength from the thicker wood. It also should be cheaper. Let your supplier see the materials list. If they can provide short pieces, you might get a better price and service than if you tried to buy long lengths to cut yourself.

Plywood

You can use plywood in many thicknesses for several parts of a small building. Sheets are mostly 4 × 8 feet, so it is wise to scheme building parts to use sheets whole or to cut them economically.

Any wood that can have the log rotated and peeled into thin veneers can be made into plywood. Much of the available plywood is made of Douglas fir, which is satisfactory for buildings, but many other woods are available, some of which have a better appearance and take paint or finish better.

Plywood is available in grades determined mostly by appearance. Prices can vary considerably, and there is no point in paying for plywood free from knots in both surface veneers if one side will be hidden.

More important is the purpose for which you intend to use the plywood. Today, most glues used in plywood have a good resistance to moisture, but this is not always true. *General-purpose plywood* might be suitable only for indoor use. However, if the inside of a small building will get wet, it is better to avoid general-purpose plywood. *External plywood* has a waterproof glue, which makes it a good choice for the construction of small buildings. *Marine-grade plywood* is even better quality than external plywood, as the plies and their arrangement, as well as the glue, suit boat-building. Marine-grade plywood costs more, though, and external plywood will do the job for your small building projects.

Particleboard

As its name implies, particleboard is made of particles or chips of wood embedded in a resin. Boards are the same size as plywood. For our purpose, it should not be less than 3/4 inch thick for strength and stiffness. You can saw it and plane it, but it is unsuitable for cutting joints.

Most particleboard will suffer if exposed to moisture, so it is unsuitable for outside use, even when you paint it.

Particleboard will make good floors. With its large, overall coverage, it might be better in your building than a floor made of many comparatively narrow boards. Similarly, it makes good one-piece shelves, but would not be suitable in a greenhouse or another place where it would be wet for long periods.

You can nail or screw particleboard. For nails near an edge, it is advisable to drill undersized holes, to avoid breaking out. For screwing into particleboard, a tapping-size hole should be taken as far as the thread will go. A screw will not cut its own way to the full depth, as it will in wood.

Hardboard

Hardboard is made from compressed wood fibers, and the sheets commonly available have one very smooth side and a patterned, opposite side. Sheets are the same size as plywood, but the thickness is only 1/8 inch.

The quality of hardboard available varies tremendously, and is largely dependent on its density. Some of it is little better than cardboard and will disintegrate in a similar way if you allow it to become wet. This hardboard, and even the better-quality, general-purpose hardboard, is unsuitable for use in a small building, except possibly for backs of cupboards or bottoms of drawers in the furnishings of the building. You could use it as a lining, when there is insulation material between it and the outer covering, but the oil-tempered type would be better.

Hardboard might be treated so it has an oil impregnation that gives it a resistance to water. It is not waterproof if subjected to moisture for a long period. Trade names vary, but there is usually something in the name to indicate "oil-tempered." You can use oil-tempered hardboard for the outside surface of a building, but you must paint it constantly. Better coverings are available.

You can obtain hardboard sheets already perforated with a pattern of small holes, probably called *peg board* or something similar. This material is not usually oil-tempered. You can buy a variety of metal clips to hook into these holes, turning the board into a great tool rack. Peg board also will make a ventilated lining, but hardboard has only limited use in a better small building.

Insulation

For many purposes, it might not be necessary to consider insulation for a small building. If it is just a storage place for garden tools, the inside temperature might not be important. If it is a workshop for year-round use, you will want to keep a comfortable temperature whatever the condition is outside.

Wood in itself provides some insulation—better than metal or solid plastic. If you have wood outside and wood or hardboard lining, the air between the two also will provide a temperature barrier. You can improve this barrier by adding one of the insulation materials used in home buildings, such as fiberglass.

Wall insulation will be helpful, but roof insulation is important and not so easy to provide. Because heat rises, much of it could escape through an uninsulated roof. A lining could hold insulation material directly under the roof, or you might fit a ceiling with insulation material above it. A wooden floor, providing the wind cannot blow under it, might be its own sufficient insulation.

Precautions to keep heat in will work in reverse, too, if keeping cool is your problem. You can then have plenty of open windows and doors to increase ventilation. Whether heat or cold is your problem, ventilation is important, otherwise your building could suffer from condensation. Arrange ventilators low and high so air can circulate. You can create a pattern of holes with flaps to cover, if the breeze is in the wrong direction, or you want to keep out rodents.

Wooden Sections

Most of the wood you use in a small building will be plain, rectangular sections and in stock sizes. For covering, you can buy boards that provide weatherproofing, even if they expand and contract. If the boards are to shed water, arrange them horizontally so they overlap. Simple weatherboarding has a tapered section (FIG. 2-1A). Clapboard has the tapered section, and shiplap board is parallel (FIG. 2-1B). Both have rabbets so boards can be fitted to lay flat on their supports. The name *shiplap* comes from the similarity to the way planks are laid in lapstrake boat building.

If you are to lay the boards vertically, you can use tongue-and-groove joints. A plain joint is not as attractive as some others. If the wood shrinks, the gaps are very obvious (FIG. 2-1C). You can make this gap less obvious with chamfers (FIG. 2- 1D). Another form that disguises the gap has a bead (FIG. 2-1E). Doors are usually made with vertical boards, even if the wall cladding is horizontal.

The window surround must protect wall-covering boards. In particular, rain must not run behind the boards. At the bottom, there should be a sill with its top sloping to shed water, and, underneath, there should be a groove to prevent water from running back (FIG. 2-1F). Stock sections are available.

Window glass is fitted best between wood fillets or into a rabbet. If you do not prepare your own, you can buy a stock section. This section might be molded also (FIG. 2-1G). You might be able to find a similar section for a door surround and another for a door step. Unfortunately, some stock sections are meant for

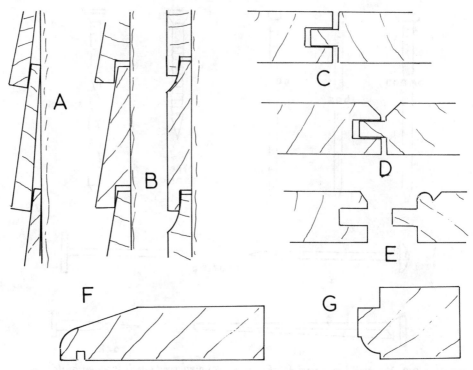

Fig. 2-1. Arrange or join boards in several ways to provide weatherproofness (A,B, C,D,E). A groove under a sill stops water from running underneath (F). You can mold a section with a rabbet (G).

home building and might be too big for a small, wooden building. Check what is available locally, and you might be able to plan details of your building to use these standard pieces.

Nailing

In many parts of your small building projects, you might not need to do anything more elaborate than put one piece of wood on top of another and nail it there. Occasionally, screws might be more suitable than nails. Usually there is no need for glue as well as nails, but a waterproof glue will strengthen the joint. Anything less than a fully waterproof glue would have only a brief life.

For most assemblies, you can use common or box nails. If you want the heads to be less prominent or if you want to punch them below the surface, casing or flooring nails with small heads are available. Their grip is not as strong, so you need more of them. For increased hold in the lower piece of wood, *ringshank* or *barbed-ring* nails are available. Another increased-hold nail has a twisted shank. For corrugated roofing, you can use nails with special heads or other roofing nails made with large heads (FIG. 2-2).

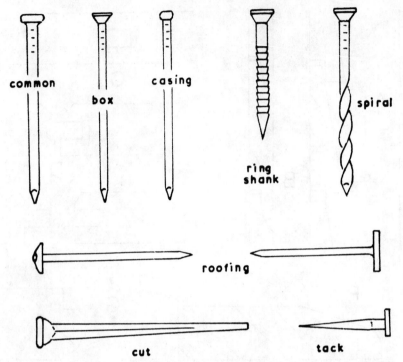

Fig. 2-2. You will use a variety of nails in constructing small wooden buildings.

Driving a nail has a splitting action on the wood fibers. In most positions, this splitting is not enough to matter, but near an end or when using very large nails, it is best to drill before driving. You should drill deep enough to clear, or almost clear, the top piece, and you need to drill an undersized hole in the lower piece (FIG. 2-3A). An increased grip comes from driving nails at alternate slight angles (FIG. 2-3B) to give a dovetail effect. This technique of driving nails with increased grip should be used only when you are certain the joint will never have to be pulled apart. Levering the joint open then might break out fibers or split the wood.

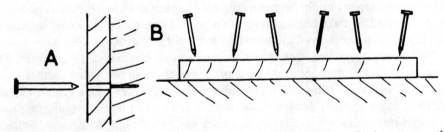

Fig. 2-3. Drill for nails to avoid splitting (A). Dovetail nailing (B) is stronger than straight nailing.

Most often, nails are made of steel, and these will probably be your choice for general construction of a building. Keep in mind, though, that steel will rust. It might not rust enough to matter, but nails in very wet conditions can rust away completely. Rust also might come through the paint and leave brown spots or streaks. You can purchase steel nails that are protected by *galvanizing* (coating with zinc) or other corrosion-resistant metals.

Aluminum nails will not corrode enough to matter. Stainless-steel nails are good to use, but they are very expensive. If you are nailing through metal, it is better to use nails of the same metal to prevent any electrolytic action between different metals, which causes corrosion. This corrosion might happen with aluminum guttering.

Screws and Bolts

Common, flat-head, wood screws are the alternatives to nails in some circumstances. Other types might be more appropriate to hinges or other metal attachments. In some buildings, there is a need for very large screws. You then need a *lag* or *coach screw*, which has a head to suit a wrench (FIG. 2-4A). Drill for it, and start it with a blow from a hammer.

Screws are made in at least as many different metals as nails, and you can buy them with various protective coatings. Galvanizing tends to be rough, which might be an advantage because of its increased grip if you are dealing with large sections of rough wood, such as posts.

Bolts are obtainable in many forms and sizes. In general, if you ask for a bolt, it is threaded to take a nut only part of its length. If you want it threaded almost to the head, you must ask for a screw. General-purpose machine bolts have square or hexagonal heads and nuts (FIG. 2-4B). Stove bolts are long and thin with screwdriver heads (FIG. 2-4C).

The bolts most useful in small buildings are coach or carriage bolts (FIG. 2-4D). Under the shallow-domed head is a square neck that pulls into the wood and prevents the bolt from turning as you tighten the nut. It also retains the bolt in the wood, although you can knock it out if you have to. This characteristic is valuable if you want to disassemble occasionally. Always use a large washer under nuts on softwood.

For attaching wood to masonry, you have a choice of methods. This choice is particularly true on the foundations. The first way is to set special bolts in the concrete as you lay it, or even use an ordinary bolt with a large washer under its head to grip the concrete (FIG. 1-4C). The other way is to drill downwards, using a fastener or plug that will grip the concrete. With the first method, you have to carefully locate the wood over bolt ends already there. In the second method, you can drill downwards through the wood, so exact positioning is not so important.

Sometimes wooden blocks are let into the concrete (FIG. 2-4E), but they should be rot-resistant wood or you might find that the attachment to the foundation is negligible if the wood is weakened by rot.

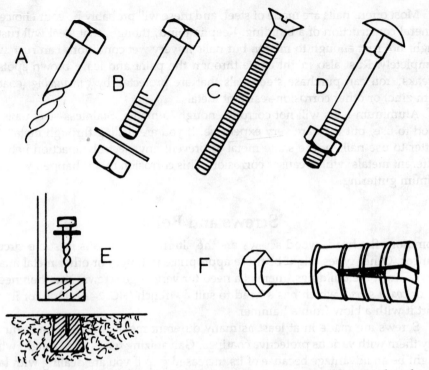

Fig. 2-4. *You need large screws and bolts for joining parts of buildings and anchoring them to their foundations.*

Methods of attaching downward into concrete involve drilling fairly large holes, for which you will need special equipment. Several types of anchors are available. They have a part that goes into the hole which is then expanded by driving a bolt or screw into it. A typical anchor has a body in two parts. When you drive a bolt in, you force the parts outward (FIG. 2-4F).

Joints

In some frames it might be strong enough to simply nail joints where parts meet (FIG. 2-5A and B). If you cannot nail from outside, you could nail diagonally inside (FIG. 2-5C). To ensure exact location, you could nail a guide block at one or both sides of a nailed joint (FIG. 2-5D).

For more exact positioning when nailing, you could cut shallow notches at corners (FIG. 2-5E) or at intermediate positions (FIG. 2-5F). These aids to accuracy are important at doorways and at window openings.

For stronger joints, you can halve the parts together, whether at corners (FIG. 2-5G), intermediately (FIG. 2-5H) or where parts cross (FIG. 2-5J).

All of these joints should be satisfactory when you can expect some strength from the covering, but if the framework has to be strong, you can use open mor-

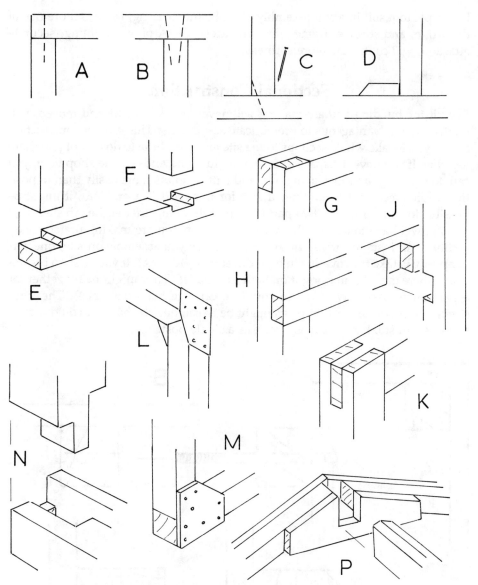

Fig. 2-5. Nail joints in framing or hold them with cut joints.

tise-and-tenon or bridle joints (FIG. 2-5K) at corners or intermediately. Nailed joints can be strengthened with sheet metal on both sides (FIG. 2-5L) or with a plywood gusset on the side away from the covering (FIG. 2-5M).

Corners of rabbeted frames, as in windows, are better joined with haunched mortise-and-tenon joints (FIG. 2-5N). For a three-way joint, as at the ridge, you can make a gusset for the third piece (FIG. 2-5P) or support it on a rail.

A framework clad with plywood contributes strength, and frame joints can be simple to result in a stiff assembly. With board covering, there is more risk of distortion, and stronger frame joints are advisable. A plywood lining, securely attached, will contribute more stiffness.

Sectional Construction

Even if the building you are making will never be taken apart and moved, you might find it advantageous to prefabricate some parts. This type of construction allows you to take whole sections to the site and have little to do except join them together. If you have the space to assemble sides and ends on the shop floor, you can do squaring, accurate laying out, and cutting joints more easily than in position while erecting the building. If size for transport is a problem, it might be possible to make a side in two parts and bolt them together at the job site.

You will have to use a little more wood when you are making prefabricated sections. For instance, if you make everything as you assemble on-site, one corner post will take the covering in both directions (FIG. 2-6A). If you wish to prefabricate, there must be an upright on both assemblies. They might nail together for a permanent assembly, or there could be carriage bolts (FIG. 2-6B). The extra strength from double corner posts might be worth having, but you could reduce sections and still have them as strong as a single post.

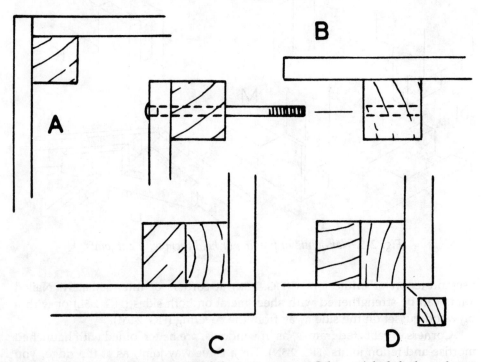

Fig. 2-6. For the simplest corners, nail them on one post. Others might bolt through two posts, with the skin overlapping or with a filler in the corner.

The covering boards could merely overlap at a corner (FIG. 2-6C), but you will protect end grain and improve the appearance when you nail in a covering strip (FIG. 2-6D).

If you have framed and boarded the roof, you might attach it in a sectional building with carriage bolts, if you arrange strips to come over the gable framing. Although you can drill holes for bolts in the roof framing or position bolts under the outer boarding, you might want to leave drilling the gables or trusses until the first assembly so that you can allow for slight variations, particularly with a ridged roof. Subsequent disassembly and re-erection will be easier if you mark all meeting parts.

When prefabricating, it is easy to accurately square door and window openings and make the fitting parts, but you might have to plane for accurate fitting after the building is in position. Even if you intend a door to reach the floor, it is advisable to make the side or end that will contain it with the bottom strip going across the opening, to keep the assembly free from twist. Cut through it after you attach the wood on each side to the floor or foundation.

3

Simple Storage Units

Several small buildings, or structures sometimes almost too small to be called buildings, might be useful on your property. A common need is for storage of garden tools, possibly some distance from your garage or main storage place, if your garden is extensive. Other items might not need much space, such as loose boating equipment near a dock or barbecue items that you prefer to keep apart from other things.

Construction is similar to any other small building, although some parts might be smaller and the work simpler. If your experience of constructing wooden buildings is slight or you are a beginning woodworker, one of these smaller assemblies will make a good introduction. It is unlikely you will go wrong, but if you do, you will not waste much material.

A very compact assembly is attractive, but make sure it will hold all you expect it to, and probably a little more. If you are preparing for garden hand tools, you do not want to have to force in something with a long handle diagonally, when you can plan for a few more inches to allow it to go in straight and cause less of an obstruction to other tools. Gather the equipment you plan to store and check to make sure you are allowing adequate internal measurements.

Walk-In Garden Shed

If a tool locker is too small for your storage needs, you can make a simple shed. It would be just big enough to walk in, but not large enough to work inside. It need not have windows and the head room might be minimal. If these are your needs, the shed in FIG. 3-1 is easy to make and the materials cost much less than for a larger building.

Fig. 3-1. *The walk-in garden shed allows you to get into the storage unit.*

The suggested sizes shown in FIG. 3-2A are for a sectional building that you can make elsewhere and assemble in position, or you can disassemble it if you wish to move it. You can use plywood completely for the cladding, or you can board the walls and the roof or make the roof of plywood. In either case, cover the roof with roofing felt or other waterproof material. Framing might be nearly all 2-inch-square sections. Board the door or make it of plywood.

The pair of ends control other sizes. Allow for the door in one end (FIGS. 3-2B and 3-3A). At the other end, the upright might be central. If the covering is plywood, it might provide sufficient strength at the corners for the framing pieces to abut against each other, but otherwise you should join them in one of the ways described in chapter 2. Locate all joints away from the corners with notches (FIG. 3-2C). Make sure the doorway will finish square. Horizontal boarding is shown in FIG. 3-2, but you could nail on vertical boards. At the high side of the door panel, put a vertical board (FIG. 3-2D). Finish the boards or plywood covering level with the framing all around.

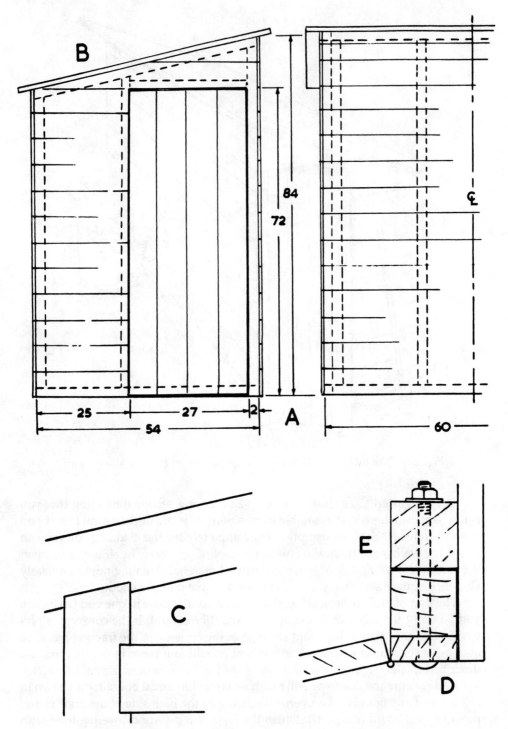

Fig. 3-2. Sizes and structural details of the walk-in garden shed.

Materials List for Walk-In Garden Shed

Ends

2 uprights	2	×	2 × 86
4 uprights	2	×	2 × 75
2 bottoms	2	×	2 × 56
2 tops	2	×	2 × 59
1 door rail	2	×	2 × 30

Back

4 uprights	2	×	2 × 75
2 rails	2	×	2 × 60

Front

4 uprights	2	×	2 × 86
2 rails	2	×	2 × 60

Roof

3 strips	2	×	2 × 54
2 panels	¾- × -35- × -66 plywood

Wall covering could be ½-inch or ¾-inch plywood or ¾-inch boards, with the lengths needed depending on widths available.

Frame the back and front in the same way, with corner and intermediate joints similar to those of the ends. Use the ends as a guide to heights, and bevel the top members of both panels to match the slope of the ends. Two intermediate uprights should provide sufficient stiffness (FIG. 3-3B).

Allow for the boards on the back and the front to overlap the ends, so the end uprights are set back sufficiently (FIG. 3-2E). Drill for 3/8-inch bolts. A bolt near the top and the bottom and two evenly spaced between the top and the bottom should be enough on each corner.

For a boarded door (FIG. 3-4A), three ledgers should be level at the hinge side but set back a little at the other side. One brace should be enough to prevent sagging. Position the top and bottom ledgers so you can screw into them from the hinges, which might be T hinges on the surface, or you can let in ordinary hinges between the door and its post. A metal loop handle would be suitable, or you could make one out of wood or turn a knob on a lathe. The simplest fastener is a strip-wood turnbutton, but you could fit a lock on the door. The door will close against the bottom framing strip. That strip might be sufficient, but you could put a short stop piece near the top as well.

The roof is larger than you can make from a normal-size, single sheet of plywood. You can have a joint at the center (FIG. 3-4B). Make the size sufficient to give an overhang of about 3 inches all around. Three strips across should fit easily between the shed back and front. Those at the ends come inside the shed

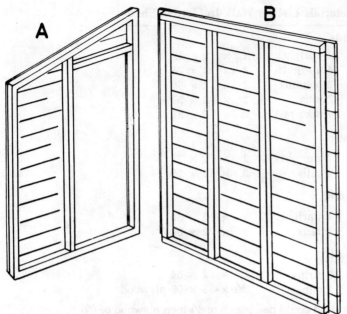

Fig. 3-3. Two walls of the walk-in garden shed.

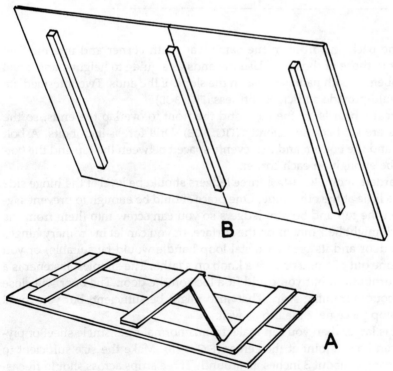

Fig. 3-4. Door and roof for the walk-in garden shed.

ends. They will hold the building square, and you should bolt them through in a similar way to the corners—three bolts on each end should be sufficient.

Although you could leave the plywood roof with just a paint finish, it would be better to cover it with a waterproof material. This covering should be the last job after you erect the building. Bolt it down to its foundation, and paint all the woodwork or treat it with preservative. For the best protection, paint inside the corners before bolting them together.

Curved-Roof Plywood Unit

Plywood has considerable strength in itself, so a building made from it needs less framing because the panels contribute plenty of stiffness. The standard 4- × -8-foot-plywood sheets are large enough for you to complete your project with few joints. Of course, any plywood that will be exposed to the weather should be exterior grade. The quality plywood you choose depends on its purpose.

You can make a covered unit with a few sheets. The simplest unit would be with a sloping roof, but you will obtain an increase in strength and rigidity by curving the plywood. You can make the assembly in FIG. 3-5 from four sheets of $1/2$-inch or thinner plywood, with framing of 2-inch-square strips. Of course, you will not be able to walk into this building, as the doorway is only 27 inches high. You could use it for sheltering tools, equipment, or for animals. If you want to treat it like a small tent, it would be possible to sleep inside!

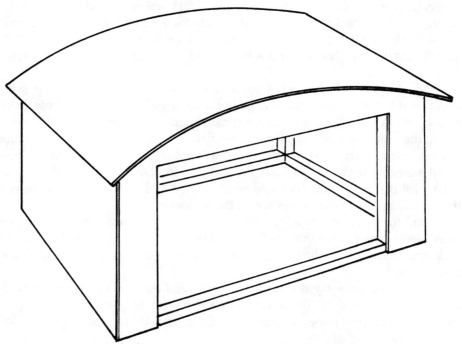

Fig. 3-5. A curved-roof unit made from sheets of plywood.

Materials List for Curved-Roof Plywood Unit

3 sheets plywood	48	×	96	× ½
3 rails	2	×	2	× 92
6 uprights	2	×	2	× 30
7 rails	2	×	2	× 44

The roof is a full sheet without cuts. The front and back are full width, but reduced in length. The ends are made from half sheets. You can complete construction quickly if you need the unit in a hurry. Making this shelter is probably quicker than any other building in this book. If you are able to spend more time on it, you can give it a better finish.

Mark out the front (FIG. 3-6A). Cut the piece to length and mark a centerline on it. You can obtain the curve of the top by bending a batten around and penciling against it, but you will get a better curve, which is part of a circle, by using an improvised compass. Have a strip of wood just over 11 feet long. At 11 feet from one end, push through an awl. Extend the centerline from the sheet and position the awl in the floor on this line so the end of the "compass" is on the edge of the center of the sheet. Pull this compass around to draw the curve with a pencil against the end. Cut the curve and use the front to mark a matching back.

When you have assembled the parts, remember to place a beveled strip across the end to take the roof (FIG. 3-6B,C). Mark where this strip goes on the front, using the actual piece of wood as a guide to size. Put a strip of wood across immediately below this beveled strip, and mark the height of the doorway (FIG. 3-6D,E). Cut out the plywood to this height and 12 inches in from the ends (FIG. 3-6F).

Put a rail across the bottom of the opening and another across the top, with uprights at the ends and at each edge of the doorway. You can nail these parts through the plywood, but for a better construction, use waterproof glue as well.

At the back, put strips at the ends and across the bottom, leaving gaps at the top corners for the beveled strips that you will put across there. Cut the end plywood pieces to match the heights of the back and front and 42 inches across (FIG. 3-6G). Nail the ends to the back and front (FIG. 3-6H). Put beveled pieces across the top edges and square pieces across the bottom edges.

Stand the assembly on a level surface and check for squareness. Put three more pieces across to hold the roof in shape (FIG. 3-6J), nailing them through the back and front and leveling them so their upper surfaces are level with the curved edges.

See that the assembly is still square, then bend the roof sheet around, with help if necessary, to check the amount of overlap at its sides and each end. Mark on it where the walls come as a guide to nailing. Start at one end to nail the roof

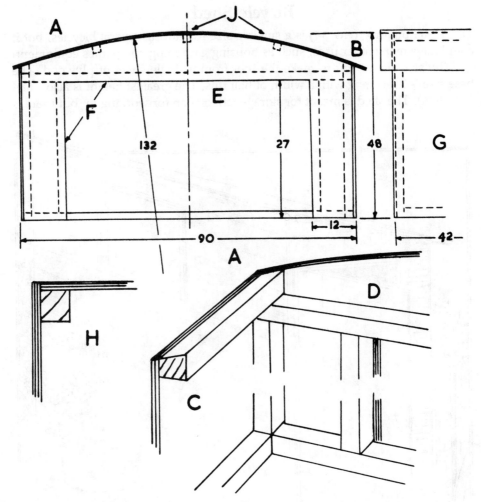

Fig. 3-6. Size and construction of the curved-roof plywood unit.

sheet down. Progress from there, nailing to each of the crosspieces in turn, until you finally nail to the beveled piece at the other end. It is the nails at the ends that are important. If you have very stiff plywood, it might be advisable to alternate screws with the nails at the ends.

You should bevel or round the corners of the roof to prevent splintering. For a better shelter, you might take off sharp edges all around. As designed, the unit goes directly on the ground. You could nail a piece of plywood to the underside of the walls to make a floor, but plywood is a better floor placed on top of the bottom-edge framing. The plywood will be easier to fit on top before you put the roof on.

Bicycle Shed

This small building (FIG. 3-7) is a suitable size for storing several bicycles, but it could have many other uses, such as housing gardening and games equipment.

The size allows you to make the roof from a single sheet of plywood. The base size is 7 feet long with a width of half this. The greatest height is also 7 feet (FIG. 3-8A). The shed is meant for storage rather than for working in, but there is

Fig. 3-7. *This small shed is a suitable size for storing several bicycles, but it could have many other uses.*

Materials List for Bicycle Shed

6 uprights	2	× 2	× 84	
6 uprights	2	× 2	× 78	
1 door upright	2	× 2	× 80	
1 door top	2	× 2	× 32	
4 wall rails	2	× 2	× 86	
4 wall rails	2	× 2	× 44	
2 window rails	2	× 2	× 30	
4 window frames	1	× 2	× 30	
4 window frames	1	× 1 1/2	× 30	
2 door frames	1	× 3 1/2	× 74	
2 door frames	1	× 3 1/2	× 32	
3 door ledgers	1	× 6	× 32	
2 door diagonals	1	× 6	× 36	
1 roof	48	× 96	× 1/2 or 3/4 plywood	
4 roof rails	2	× 2	× 44	

Covering: 1/2 plywood or shiplap boards 3/4 × 6

sufficient head room and a window to provide light. The shed is best fastened down to a concrete base, but you could stand it elsewhere and put a wood floor inside.

Most of the framing is 2-inch-square wood. The covering could be plywood, but shiplap or other boards about 6 inches wide are suggested. No lining is shown, but if the use you intend would be better with some insulation, plywood could be added to the inside of the framing. You can prefabricate all the parts before assembling on site. If you ever wish to move the shed, it should be possible to take the units apart with very little damage. The ends are covered with boards or plywood level with the uprights (FIG. 3-8B), then the sides are made with the covering extended (FIG. 3-8C) and the corners bolted together.

Start by making the end with the doorway (FIGS. 3-8D and 3-9A). Framing can be nailed, but it helps in locating parts and preventing movement if you cut shallow notches (FIG. 3-8E). Check squareness and cover with boards or plywood so all edges are level, including around the doorway. At the narrow edge beside the doorway, put a strip to make up the level of the boards.

Make the opposite end to be a pair in overall size, but use one central upright.

Assemble the frame for the front to match the height of the ends (FIGS. 3-8F and 3-9B). The top edge could be beveled to suit the slope of the roof, but the angle is slight and it might not matter if you leave this edge square. Divide the length into three equal parts for the uprights, unless you prefer a different width of window opening. Notch and nail all frame parts. Check squareness and cover the framing, allowing enough projection to fit over the end walls.

Make the back in a similar way. Compare its length with the front and its height with the lower edges of the ends. It is unlikely that you will need a win-

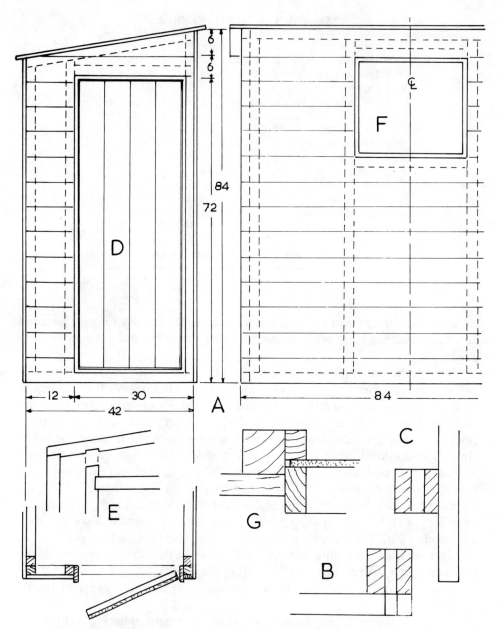

Fig. 3-8. Suggested sizes for the bicycle shed and some constructional details.

dow in the back, but you could put one there or in the end if that will suit the intended use.

Edge the window opening with strips that project about ¹/₂ inch (FIG. 3-8G), leaving space for the glass and strips inside to hold it. It will be wisest to leave

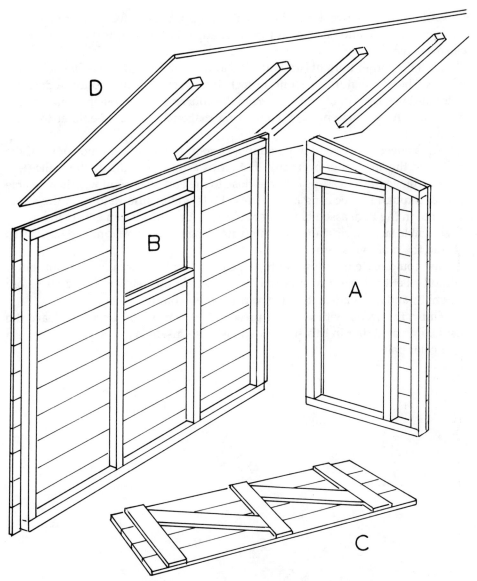

Fig. 3-9. Units that fit together to make the bicycle shed.

fitting the glass until after the shed has been erected. Edge the door opening with strips that project a little in a similar way. The bottom edge could be extended further with a supporting block underneath to form a step.

Make the door (FIG. 3-9C) to be an easy fit in the doorway. Use vertical boards or plywood and three ledgers with two diagonals sloping upwards from the hinged side. The door could be hinged either way to suit your preference. Use plenty of nails to reduce the risk of wood movement or warping later. It should be sufficient to use two 4-inch hinges at the upper and lower ledger positions. Arrange a handle and fastener at the other edge. Put a stop strip for the door to close against.

Drill the corner uprights for bolts. It should be sufficient to use $3/8$-inch bolts, with washers and nuts at about 18-inch intervals. Drill the bottom edges for holding-down bolts or other fasteners to the concrete. Assemble the four walls in position. Check squareness by comparing diagonal measurements at top and bottom.

Try a sheet of plywood in position as a roof. Mark on it the positions of the walls and the amount of overhang. Put strips across to fit inside the walls (FIG. 3-9D). Arrange the end strips to come close to the end walls. You will then be able to drill through for securing bolts. These bolts will ensure rigidity of the structure, but in the final assembly you should nail (or screw if you expect to have to disassemble later) at close enough intervals along the tops of front and back walls to hold the roof joints tight.

You could leave the plywood top uncovered and protect it with paint, but it would be better covered with tarred felt. If you do this, stiffen the edges before assembly, and add battens to the covering when you fit it.

Finish the wood with paint or preservative. You might decide to leave the inside untreated, but in this small shed visibility inside is improved if you use a light-color paint.

4

Shelters

People need shelters for many occasions. The shelters I am referring to are not fully enclosed buildings with doors. They usually have one or more sides open. In a garden or yard, such a shelter might be all you need for storing yard furniture. You can add seating to the shelter so you can rest from your labors or sit and admire the flowers growing. Anyone collecting admission money at an event can use a simple shelter, possibly of portable construction. Something similar might provide shelter for children waiting for the school bus.

A more advanced shelter could have an enclosed part with door and windows towards the back and a broad, more open part, large enough for chairs and table, at the front. You might call this type shelter a summerhouse or a gazebo. If made large enough, it almost could become a second home. It is difficult to decide on the dividing line between a shelter and a building.

Construction might be very similar to some of the buildings described in chapter 3, but if the front is open, there is a problem of providing stiffness there. If you provide the open front by just leaving out what would be the front of the building, there is no crosswise stiffness, and a hard push or even a strong wind on one side could distort or even collapse the shelter.

Sun Shelter

Something with a more decorative appearance than the rather basic take-down shelter will look better in a yard or garden if you intend to sit in it, sheltered from wind and sun. You can also use it to store outdoor furniture or garden tools.

As shown in FIG. 4-1, the back and the front are parallel and upright, but the side walls slope inwards. Curve the top and back of the door opening, and give the front bargeboards shaped edges to avoid an austere appearance. This design includes a wooden floor, so the shelter could be self-contained and not attached to the ground, making it easier to move it to a different location. With the usual softwood construction, it should be possible for two men to carry the whole assembly for a short distance.

The sizes suggested in FIG. 4-2A allow for occupying a ground area about 48 inches × 60 inches, but you can modify the sizes to suit your needs, providing you do not increase the size excessively. The skin suggested is shiplap boarding, but you can use plywood or other sheet material. You can use boards or plywood

Fig. 4-1. The sun shelter has sloping sides and decorative bargeboards.

Materials List for Sun Shelter

8 uprights	2	× 2	× 75
1 upright	2	× 2	× 86
4 tops	2	× 2	× 30
2 bottoms	2	× 2	× 62
2 bottoms	2	× 2	× 50
2 bottom supports	2	× 2	× 50
2 top rails	2	× 2	× 50
4 corners	1	× 1	× 75
2 roofs	36- × -72- x-¾ plywood (or boards)		
4 roof edges	1½ × 1½ × 36		
2 roof edges	1½ × 1½ × 74		
1 ridge	2	× 4	× 50
4 bargeboards	¾ × 5	× 36	
2 bargeboard ends	¾ × 4	× 15	
1 floor	48- × -60- × -¾ plywood or particle board (or boards)		

Covering: shiplap boards about ¾ × 6

for the roof, then cover it with roofing felt or other material. Nail the bargeboards on after you have covered the roof. You can build in any seating or you can rely on separate chairs.

The key assembly is the back (FIG.4-3A). Set this part of the building out symmetrically about a centerline. With the usual covering, one central upright should be all that you need to supplement the outside framing, which you can halve together (FIG. 4-3B). Cover the back with boarding, working from the bottom up.

Use the back as a pattern for getting the shape of the front (FIG. 4-3C). Arrange uprights for the doorway sides. Cover with boarding. At the top of the opening, nail stiffening pieces inside and cut the curve through them and the boarding, preferably with a jigsaw. Round all edges of the doorway.

You can make the two sides as separate units, with bolts into the back and the front, if you want to prefabricate the shelter or arrange it to take apart for removal to another site, but it is compact enough for you to move it bodily by truck. Consequently, you might find it simpler to assemble it completely and permanently. If so, put pieces across at top and bottom and central uprights at each side (FIG. 4-3D).

The easiest way to join to the front and back is with sheet-metal gussets. When you have nailed the side boarding on, you will strengthen the joints further. For the neatest corners, stop the board ends at the uprights and fill the corners with square strips (FIG. 4-2B).

You might consider it satisfactory for your purpose for the eaves strips to be left with square edges, but it will be better to plane them to the slope of the roof (FIG. 4-2C) and make a ridge piece with matching slopes (FIG. 4-2D).

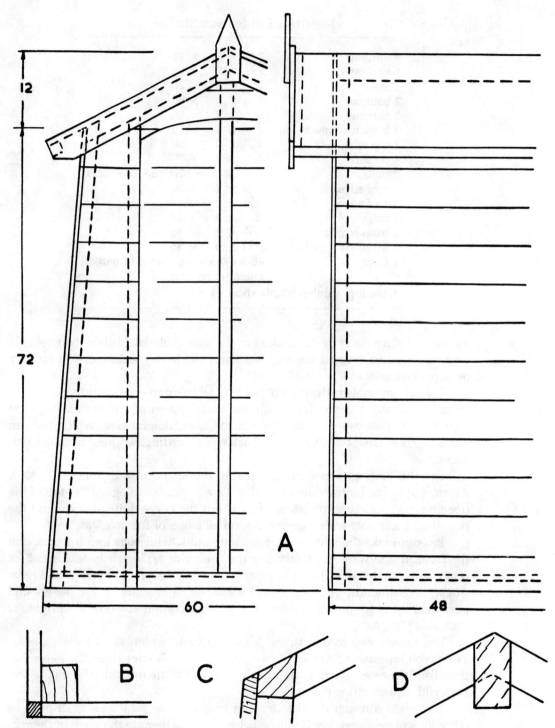

Fig. 4-2. *Sizes and corner joints of the sun shelter.*

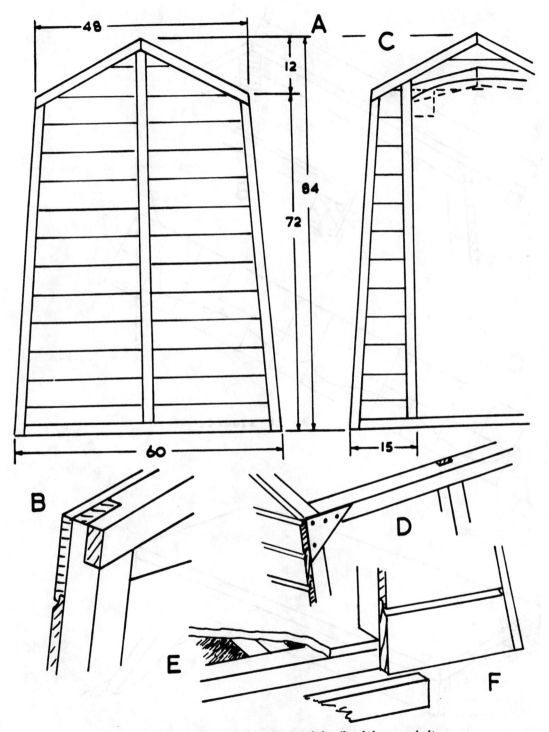

Fig. 4-3. Back, front, and constructional details of the sun shelter.

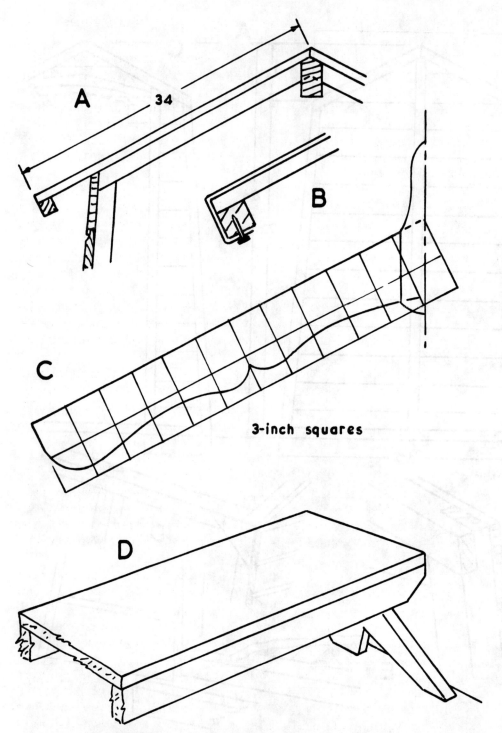

Fig. 4-4. Roof, bargeboard, and seat details for the sun shelter.

Square the assembly as you fit the floor. What stiffening you provide depends on the materials. Two pieces from back to front should be sufficient (FIG. 4-3E). Over these strips might come particleboard, plywood, or 6-inch-wide boards. Cover the front edge with a strip to match the thickness of the shiplap boarding (FIG. 4-3F).

Allow for a 6-inch roof overhang all around. You can use plywood or arrange boards from back to front. Stiffen all edges with strips below (FIG. 4-4A). Take the roof-covering material over the top without joints. Turn in the edges and tack underneath (FIG. 4-4B). Use more large-head nails elsewhere on the roof, if necessary.

Make the bargeboards to stand about $1/2$ inch above the roof covering and to project at least 1 inch at the eaves. Leave the lower edges straight, or give them a regular pattern of deckle edges. The pattern shown is distinctive (FIG. 4-4C), and you can cut it with a portable jigsaw. Cut one and use it as a pattern for marking the others. The central piece can have a simple point, or it can be curved to match the other decoration.

If you put strips across the sides at seat height, you can place one or more boards across as a seat and move them to stand on end if you want to use the shelter as a store. Another idea would be to make a bench with its feet arranged to come between the sides (FIG. 4-4D); then you can lift outside when you prefer the open air.

If the sun shelter is to stand on soil or grass, soak the lower parts (at least) with preservative. For a permanent position, you should place it on a concrete base. You can leave the inside untreated, but it would look best if you finished it in a light-color paint, even if you paint the outside in a dark color.

Ridged-Canopied Shelter

A ridged roof has a more attractive appearance than a lean-to or single slope. Both look better than a horizontal roof. Over a certain size, a ridged roof is preferable, as it sheds rain and snow easier and offers less wind resistance. A shelter with a ridge from back to front and extending canopy or porch has good access, provides maximum shelter, and looks good.

The shelter in FIG. 4-5 has a floor area of about 60 inches by 84 inches, with a lengthwise canopy of approximately another 24 inches. Good clearance is provided through the doorway, and the shelter has ample head room inside. No base or floor is shown, but you could add a wooden or concrete platform, or you might build in a wooden floor. Construction is sectional, so you can prefabricate most parts and bolt them together on-site.

Shiplap boarding is suggested for the covering, but you can use other materials. The sizes given in FIG. 4-6A allow for economical cutting of standard plywood sheets. Arrange internal framing of some panels to suit joints between plywood sheets. Join framing parts to each other by halving, tenoning, or by using sheet-metal gussets. Many parts will be satisfactory if you notch and nail them.

Fig. 4-5. This canopied shelter has a ridged roof.

Materials List for Ridged-Canopied Shelter

14 uprights	2	× 2	×	80
2 uprights	2	× 2	×	104
5 rails	2	× 2	×	92
4 rails	2	× 2	×	56
4 edge covers	1	× 3	×	80
2 corners	1	× 1	×	80
10 roof frames	1½	× 1½	×	60
2 roof frames	1½	× 1½	×	90
2 bargeboards	1	× 6	×	60
8 roof battens	½	× 1½	×	60
Shiplap boards for walls 1 × 6 (approximately)				
Roof: 1- × -10 boards or ¾ plywood				

Start by making the front (FIG. 4-7A). Fit this piece between the sides, and allow the covering boards to extend to overlap the side uprights. The doorway is shown 48 inches wide, but you can alter that. If you want good protection for articles stored inside, make it narrower. If you want to let in plenty of sunlight while you sit inside, make it wider.

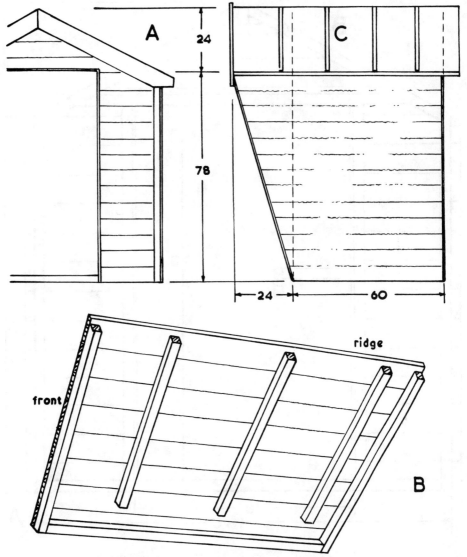

Fig. 4-6. Sizes and roof details for the ridged-canopied shelter.

At the top, cut away for a 2-inch-×-4-inch ridge piece to pass through and put a supporting piece across, below the gap (FIG. 4-7B). After covering with boards, put rounded-edge pieces at each side of the doorway (FIG. 4-7C).

The back has the same outline as the front. Bolt its uprights to the uprights at the rear of the sides, and cut the boarding to allow for fitting a square strip in the corner. To allow for fully boarding the back, arrange two uprights to the full height intermediately (FIG. 4-7D).

Make the pair of sides (FIG. 4-8A), cutting the boards level with the framing.

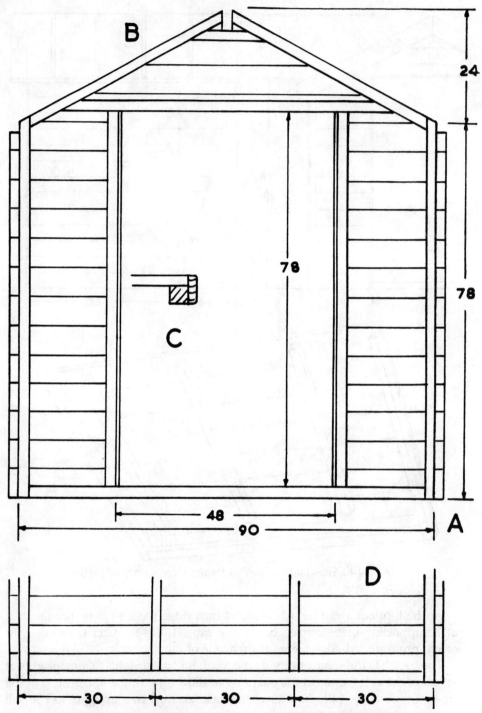

Fig. 4-7. Front and back details for the ridged-canopied shelter.

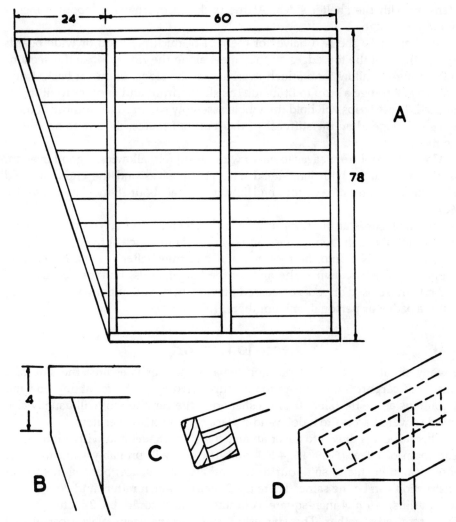

Fig. 4-8. Side and roof details for the ridged-canopied shelter.

Allow a 4-inch vertical part at the front to take the bargeboards. Reinforce with a block inside (FIG. 4-8B). Check the side heights against the matching parts of the front and back. Bevel the top edges to suit the slope of the roof. Cover the front sloping edges for a neat finish (FIG. 4-8C).

For assembly, it should be satisfactory to use ³/₈-inch coach bolts at about 18-inch intervals. Drill holes for these bolts in the sides. Do not continue drilling into the front and back uprights until you bring them together on-site, to ensure exact mating of holes.

Make a 2-inch-×-4-inch ridge piece to go right through the full length of the roof. Bevel its top edge to match the slope on each side. At the front, match the extension with the shelter sides. At the back, an overhang of about 5 inches should be enough.

You can make the two halves of the roof of thick plywood or wide boards (FIG. 4-6B). Bevel the top edges so they meet along the ridge. Make the sections wide enough to allow for a 5-inch overhang at the sides. Frame at back, front, and eaves. Arrange a strip to fit inside the shelter front and another to fit inside the back. These strips will hold the whole assembly square. The number of other pieces will depend on the stiffness of the roof, but there will have to be at least one more.

Cover the roof from eaves to eaves with tarred felt, allowing a good overlap. Turn under and fix with large-head nails at the eaves and the ends. To hold down the fairly large area on top, nail light battens at about 18-inch intervals (FIG. 4-6C).

Fit bargeboards at the front only, or at both ends. Cut so the boards stand about 1 inch above the roof surface and overlap about 1 inch at the corners of the roof (FIG. 4-8D). Nail into the roof end and into the shelter's sides. No central, decorative piece is shown at the apex of the bargeboards, but you can use one similar to those used on roofs discussed previously, or you might wish to cut and mount a badge or personal emblem there.

Lean-To Carport

In many situations, the best position for a car shelter is against the side of a house. The carport is then a lean-to roof supported by the house at one side and by columns at the free side. Besides sheltering the car, the roof will usually also provide covered access to a door and a place to protect smaller items.

This carport is drawn to cover an area 9 feet by 18 feet and with a minimum head room of 7 feet (FIGS. 4-9, 4-10, and 4-11). You will probably want to adapt these measurements to suit your needs and available space, but the method of construction can be the same. There are 2-inch-×-6-inch rafters and 2-inch-×-4-inch purlins, with 4-inch-square columns, which could be 2-inch-×-4-inch pieces screwed together. The suggested roof is translucent plastic corrugated sheeting, but you could use corrugated metal or fit plywood sheets to cover with felt.

Start by drawing the main lines of the slope of the roof (FIG. 4-10A). This will give you the length of the rafters and the angle of some parts. The two beams (FIG. 4-10B and C) are best beveled on the top edges, but the slope is slight and you should find it satisfactory to leave these edges square. Cut the two beams to length, and mark on them the positions of the rafters (FIG. 4-11A). Make the seven rafters 6 inches deep. Allow for halving joints at their ends (FIG. 4-10D). Cut the purlins to the same length as the beams (FIG. 4-11B) and mark on the positions of the rafters. If you have to use shorter lengths, allow for joints over rafters. Thicken the rafters where the joints will come, to permit a longer cut end of each

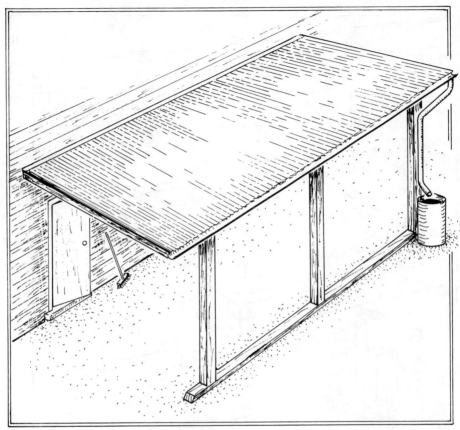

Fig. 4-9. *A lean-to carport can be built onto the side of a building or existing wall.*

Materials List for
Lean-To Carport

3 columns	4	× 4	×	92
2 beams	2	× 6	×	216
7 rafters	2	× 6	×	112
3 purlins	2	× 4	×	216
1 base strip	2	× 4	×	200

purlin (FIG. 4-10E). If there are to be several of these joints, stagger them, so they come on different rafters.

Cut halving joints where all roof parts cross (FIG. 4-11C), so top surfaces will come level. If you have not beveled the beams, make the joints so the rafters will finish level with the outer edges of the beams; then you will get the best fit of roofing material.

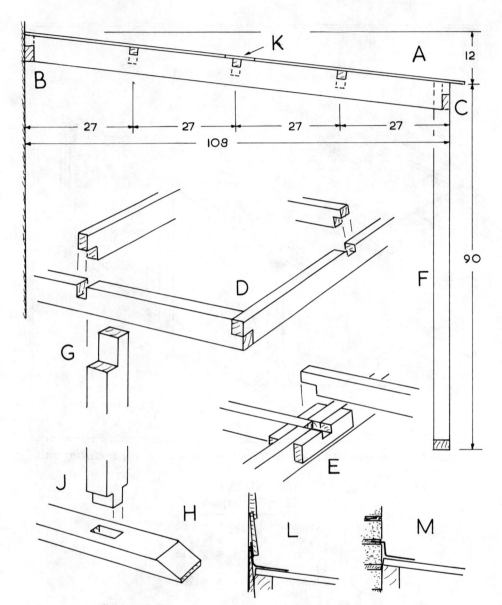

Fig. 4-10. End view and constructional details for the lean-to carport.

The three columns are the same. Cut them to length to reach the top surface of the beam (FIG. 4-10F). You will probably mount them on concrete or other hard surface, but they could be lengthened to go into the ground. Notch the tops to fit around the beam (FIG. 4-10G) When you assemble, the notches will be located on the outsides of the rafters (FIG. 4-11D).

Make a base strip to extend about 12 inches past the end columns (FIG. 4-10H) with beveled ends. Mark mortises for the columns and form tenons to match

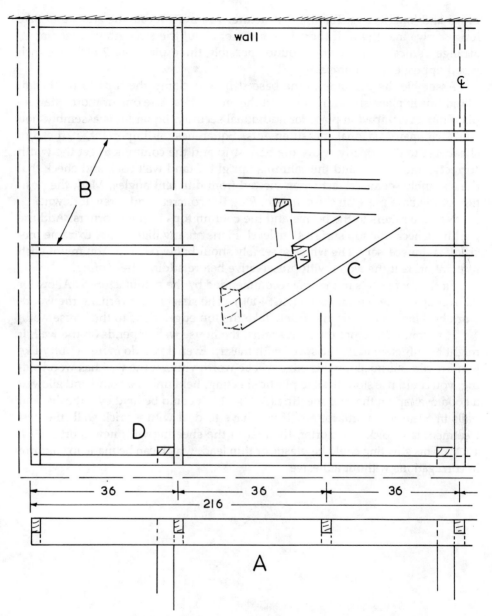

Fig. 4-11. *Roof details for the lean-to carport.*

(FIG. 4-10J). To allow for adjustment to get the columns plumb during assembly, you could cut the mortises too long and fill any spaces with wood after satisfactory assembly.

The top beam has to be held to the side of the house securely. How this is done will depend on the house structure. With brick or stone, there should be plugs and long screws. For wood structure, you must locate the studs and take long screws into them. If there is any doubt about the strength of attachment, arrange vertical strips to the ground, possibly three pieces of 2-inch-×-4-inch wood opposite the columns.

Assemble the columns to the base strip and clamp the tops to the beam. Stand this in place and temporarily fit the end rafters. Use one or more intermediate rafters clamped in place for additional security. Square this assembly. You could compare diagonal measurements. Squareness is important, if the roof sheets are to fit properly. Move the base strip and the columns to get the width correct at the bottom and the columns upright. Stand well back and check that the assembly seems correct when viewed from different angles. Mark the position of the base piece on the concrete. Plug the concrete and screw it down.

Nail the rafters to the beams and the column tops in their corners. Add the purlins. Check that top surfaces are level. Plane off any high spots. Extreme precision is unnecessary. The whole assembly should now be rigid. You might wish to paint or treat the wood with preservative before adding the roofing.

Fit the roof sheets in the way recommended by the manufacturers. Allow for an overlap on the central purlin (FIG. 4-10K) . The sheets can overhang the woodwork by 3 inches at ends and front. Take the top edges close to the house wall.

How you waterproof the joint against the house wall depends on the wall. It might be sufficient to fill the space with mastic. Even if you do more, a putty-like jointing compound along this edge will be worthwhile. If the wall has wood siding, you could use stout flexible plastic sheeting, held under a board and allowed a good overlap on the roof sheeting (FIG. 4-10L). It could be held by adhesive and nails into the beam and rafters. If you have to deal with a brick wall, the best treatment is to pick out mortar, then let in the sheeting with new mortar (FIG. 4-10M). This sheeting could be plastic or thin lead, which can be made to conform to corrugations without adhesive.

5

Workshops

A workshop away from the house allows you to carry on your hobby, even if it is noisy and dirty, without affecting other people. You also do not have to clear things away after a working session.

Such a workshop should be large enough and strong enough, with adequate natural lighting. A concrete base is advisable, but a wood floor is more comfortable and kinder to dropped tools. Your practical needs are most important, but do not overlook appearance. You want this building to look attractive and to fit in with its surroundings.

Basic Workshop

The size and arrangement of a building you make for use as a hobby shop will depend on many factors, including the available space and the situation. You will have to consider the actual craft or occupation and its needs. However, a building with about an 8-foot-×-12-foot floor area with working head room and several windows will suit woodworking and metalworking, as well as many other crafts. The building shown in FIG. 5-1 is of basic, partly prefabricated construction. It has a door wide enough to pass most pieces of furniture or light machinery, and the suggested windows should give enough light if most activities are on a bench you arrange at one long side.

At the entrance end, a window is shown in the door. The wall alongside it then would be available for shelves and racks. Two windows, which open, are shown over the long bench (FIG. 5-2A), and you might put another window which opens at the back (FIG. 5-2B). Besides providing ventilation, these win-

Materials List for Basic Workshop

Ends

5 uprights	2	× 3	×	80
2 uprights	2	× 3	×	100
3 uprights	2	× 3	×	90
4 rails	2	× 3	×	98
4 tops	2	× 3	×	54

Sides

10 uprights	2	× 3	×	80
8 rails	2	× 3	×	138
4 corners	1	× 2	×	80

Cladding

1- × -6 shiplap boards or ¾ plywood

Door

2 frames	1	× 4	×	80
1 frame	1	× 4	×	40
3 ledges	1	× 6	×	38
1 brace	1	× 6	×	45
7 boards	1	× 6	×	80
2 window sides	1	× 2	×	16
4 window frames	1	× 2½	×	16
8 window fillets	1	× 1	×	16

Windows

6 frames	1	× 4½	×	20
3 frames	1	× 4½	×	36
1 sill	1	× 5½	×	36
1 sill	1	× 5½	×	74
6 stops	1	× 1½	×	20
6 stops	1	× 1½	×	36
6 window sides	1½	× 1½	×	20
6 window rails	1½	× 1½	×	36

Roof

1 ridge	2	× 6	×	160
2 eaves	2	× 4	×	160
2 purlins	2	× 2	×	160
16 battens	½	× 1	×	54
2 rafters	2	× 3	×	54
1 tie	2	× 3	×	40
4 bargeboards	1	× 5	×	60
Covering	1- × -6 boards or ¾ plywood			

Fig. 5-1. A basic workshop with boarded walls and ample windows.

dows allow long or awkward work to be extended outside, if that is the only way to handle it. You might leave the other long side without windows, but that will depend on your needs. If you want to have a lathe or table saw near that wall, arrange more windows there, not necessarily ones which open.

This structure is not intended to be a portable building. It is not intended to be moved once you have assembled it fully. However, you can prefabricate much of it. You can make the four walls elsewhere, then assemble them to each other on-site and add the roof. Nearly all the framing is made from 2-inch- × -3-inch-section wood. The covering is shiplap boards about 6 inches wide, but you could use exterior plywood or other covering. As described, the building is not intended to be lined, but it would not be difficult to line and insulate the finished building. If you build in a full-length bench, it will give rigidity to the structure as well as help brace the building. Fix shelves, racks, and other storage arrangements directly to the walls.

Start by making one end (FIG. 5-3A). Halve or tenon external-frame joints. Halve or notch internal-meeting joints. Halve crossing parts. At the top, bevel the rafters to rest on the other parts and nail through. Check squareness by comparing diagonals—a door or window out of true will be very obvious.

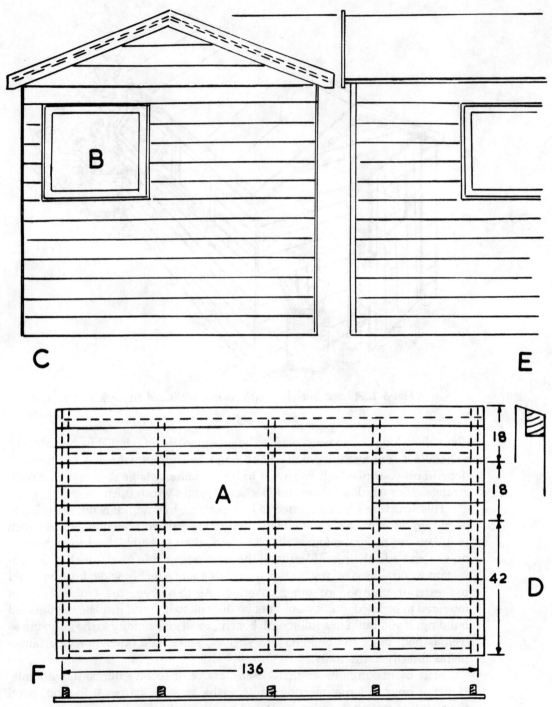

Fig. 5-2. Suggested sizes for the basic workshop.

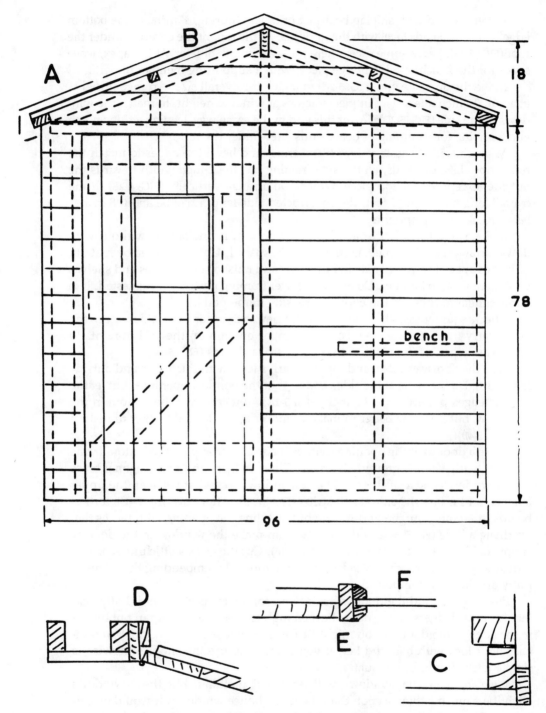

Fig. 5-3. *The door end of the workshop.*

Cover the end with shiplap boarding or other covering, starting at the bottom edge. Cut board ends level with the uprights. At the top, fit the covering under the roof (FIG. 5-3B). Leave some excess here for trimming to fit later. At the apex, leave space for the 2-inch-×-6-inch ridge piece, with a supporting member under it.

Make the opposite end (FIG. 5-2C) to match the overall size. Arrange uprights at about 24-inch intervals. Put pieces across at window height, to match the windows in the side (FIG. 5-2D). Cover this end in the same way, leaving a ridge notch and allowing for trimming of board ends later under the roof.

Make the side heights to match the ends, and bevel top edges to match the roof slope. Like the ends, all the side framing has the 2-inch width towards the outside, except for the top piece, which you arrange vertically (FIG. 5-2E). If the overall length is to be 12 feet, the constructed side length will be about 8 inches less (FIG. 5-2F) over uprights.

Make a side frame with rails for the windows. If one side is without windows, arrange two intermediate rails equally spaced. Uprights are shown about 32 inches apart, but you could alter uprights and rails to suit benches and shelves you might wish to build in. Do not have fewer framing parts than suggested. Use joints similar to those in the ends for the side frame parts.

Check squareness, then cover the framework. Where the sides meet the ends, carry the boarding over, so it will go far enough on the end uprights to allow you to put a filler piece in to cover the board ends (FIG. 5-3C).

Line the doorway sides, and top with strips level with the inside and outside (FIG. 5-3D). Do the same at the sides and tops of the window openings, but let the outside edges project up to 1/2 inch (FIG. 5-4A). You can treat the bottom in the same way, but it will be better to make it thicker and extend it further to make a sill (FIG. 5-4B).

Make a door to fit the opening, with its boards overlapping the bottom frame member, with 1/2-inch ground clearance. Three ledgers and one diagonal brace are shown in FIG. 5-5A. If there is to be a window, arrange it between the upper ledgers, and frame the sides with strips (FIG. 5-5B). After covering with vertical boards (preferably tongue-and-groove boards), line the opening with pieces that overhang a little (FIGS. 5-3E and 5-5C). You can make the window in the door by simply holding glass between strips (FIG. 5-3F). Cut the glass a little undersize, to reduce any risk of cracking. Waterproof the window by embedding the edges in putty or a jointing compound.

Put strips around the doorway sides and top to act as stops and draftproofing. Keep the ledgers on the door short enough to clear them. You can put hinges in the edge of the door, or you might fit T hinges across the surface. Fit an ordinary door lock with bolt and key, if you want to secure the shop; otherwise, a simple latch should be adequate.

You can make the windows with standard molding, but these windows might be a much lighter section than the usual house windows. It would be better to prepare simple, rabbeted strips (FIG. 5-4C). If you use a standard window

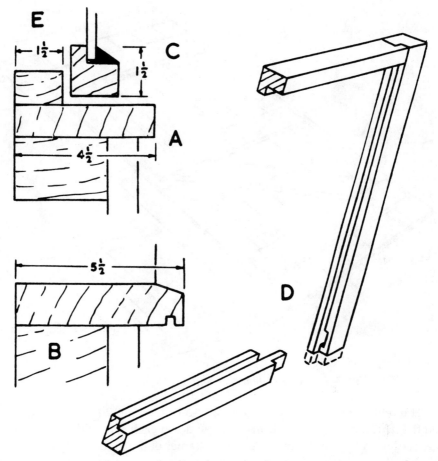

Fig. 5-4. Window details for the workshop.

molding, you probably will have to increase the width of the pieces around the window openings.

Make up the windows with mortise-and-tenon joints (FIG. 5-4D). Leave the sides too long until after assembly, to reduce the risk of end grain breaking out. Make the windows so they fit easily in their openings. Put stop strips around the inner edges of the framing (FIG. 5-4E). Hinge the windows at the top and arrange fasteners and struts inside at the bottom. You might want to lift the windows horizontally occasionally, but you can do that with a temporary strut or a cord from higher on the wall. When you are satisfied with the fit and action of a window, you can putty in the glass, although it might be better to putty after you have painted the wood. The building will look attractive if you paint the window frames and bargeboards a different color than the main parts, so you could paint the window frames and glaze them in advance of final assembly.

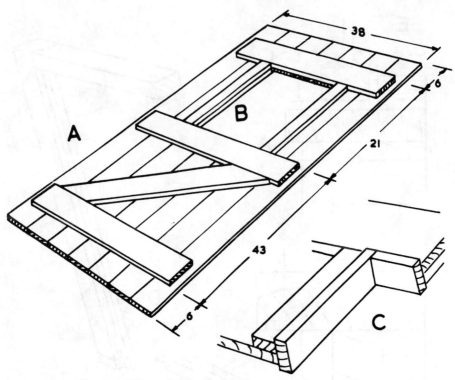

Fig. 5-5. The workshop door with a cutout for a window.

The roof is supported by the 2-inch-×-6-inch ridge, 2-inch-×-4-inch eaves laid flat, and 2-inch-square purlins halfway down each side of the roof. Nail the eaves strips and purlins to the sloping top frames of the ends and bevel the ridge to match (FIG. 5-6A). Let the ends project about 3 inches at each end of the building. Cut the shiplap-covering boards around them, and trim their top edges to match the roof (FIG. 5-6B).

On a 12-foot length, having rafters only at the center should be sufficient to prevent sagging of the roof. If you make the building longer or have doubts about the stiffness of the assembly, use two sets of rafters, spacing them equally. Cut a pair of rafters to fit between the top pieces of the side frames and the ridge (FIG. 5-6C). Check straightness of the sides while cutting. If you get the length of a rafter wrong, it could make the side bulge or bend in slightly. You can have a nailing block at one or both ends of each rafter. A block below the purlin will locate and support it (FIG. 5-6D). Put a strip across the rafters below the ridge (FIG. 5-6E). No other lower tie is needed.

You can cover the roof with exterior-grade plywood, but FIG. 5-6F shows it boarded. Finish level at the eaves. Put covering material over the structure in single lengths from one eaves to the other, if possible, turning the ends under and nailing them. Any overlaps should be wide, and you should arrange them so

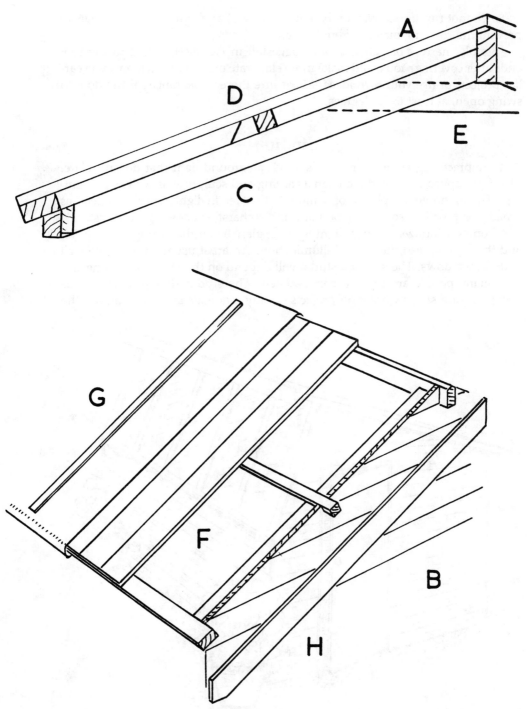

Fig. 5-6. Roof details for the workshop.

water cannot run under. Nail on battens (FIG. 5-6G) at about 18-inch intervals to prevent the covering material from lifting.

Simple, narrow bargeboards are suggested in FIG. 5-6H, nailed to the roof ends after covering. You could make more elaborate ones, as shown on some earlier projects or use your own ideas. Make sure there is clearance for the door to swing open, at least to 90 degrees.

Studio

Anyone practicing an art form needs good, all-around light that doesn't glare. This fact applies to three-dimensional carving and sculpture as well as to painting. There should be plenty of windows that let in light where needed, as broadly as possible, so there is no glare and so harsh shadows are not cast.

Sloping windows will pass light without glare better than upright windows, and they will spread the natural illumination. An artist usually wants one wall without windows. The size of a studio will depend on the work to be done and how many people are to be accommodated. The studio shown in FIG. 5-7 is designed for a single worker on projects of only moderate size. You can use the

Fig. 5-7. This studio gets good light from sloping windows.

Materials List for Studio

Ends

6 uprights	2	× 2	× 80
2 uprights	2	× 2	× 90
2 uprights	2	× 2	× 50
2 uprights	2	× 2	× 56
6 rails	2	× 2	× 98
2 tops	2	× 2	× 98

Back

5 uprights	2	× 2	× 80
3 rails	2	× 2	× 92
2 corners	1	× 1	× 80

Lower front

5 uprights	2	× 2	× 50
2 rails	2	× 2	× 92
2 corners	1	× 1	× 50

Upper front

6 uprights	2	× 2	× 56
2 rails	2	× 2	× 92
1 sill	1	× 4½	× 92
2 cover pieces	1	× 5	× 56

End window

3 frames	1	× 3½	× 34
1 sill	1	× 4½	× 34
4 frames	2	× 2	× 34

Door

3 ledgers	1	× 6	× 32
2 braces	1	× 6	× 40
6 boards	1	× 6	× 78

Roof

5 rafters	2	× 3	× 116
1 fascia	1	× 6	× 116
4 edges	1½	× 1½	× 116

Covering: boards   1- × -6 or ¾ plywood

Cladding

Shiplap boards   1- × -6 or ¾ plywood (approximately)

same construction for a studio of a different size. The suggested sizes are for an 8-foot-square floor space and the same size maximum height (FIG. 5-8). Lined walls and roof are advisable. The smooth interior, painted a light color, will help to disperse lighting evenly. Although you might use a concrete base, a wooden floor over it would be comfortable and kinder to dropped tools. Cladding is assumed to be shiplap boarding, but you could use plywood. The 8-foot-square size makes for economical use of standard plywood sheets.

Start with one side that has a door (FIG. 5-9A). You can use any of the usual framing joints at most places. Where the sloping and vertical fronts join, use a halving joint, with screws both ways (FIG. 5-9B). Cover with boards cut level at the back and front edges, but with enough left at the top to trim to the same height as the rafters (FIG. 5-9C).

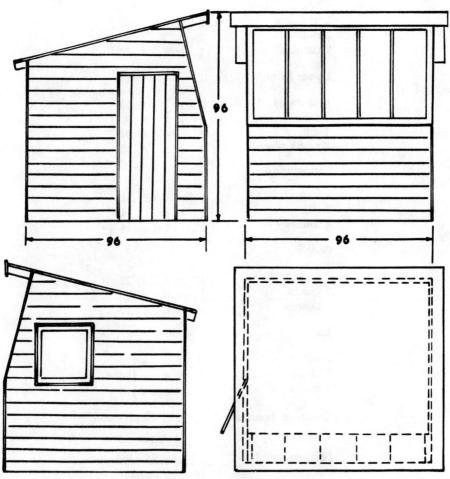

Fig. 5-8. Suggested sizes for the studio.

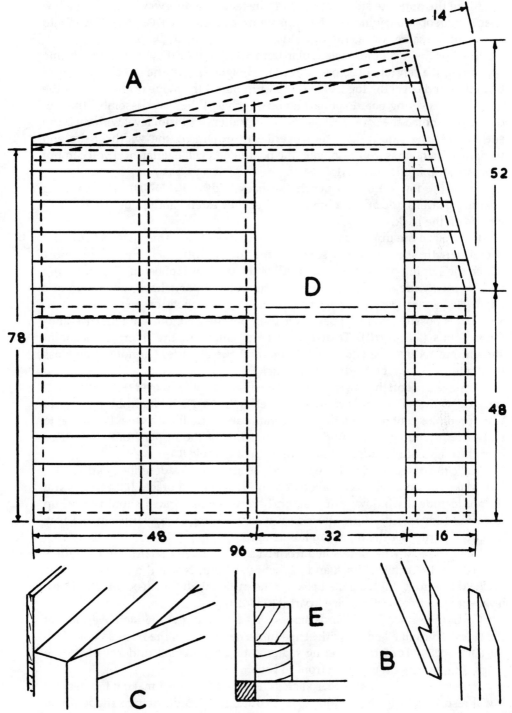

Fig. 5-9. The studio end.

Make the opposite side identical, but instead of a doorway, you could allow space for an opening window, the same width as the door (FIG. 5-9D). Cover with boards in the same way as the first side.

The back is a simple, rectangular frame (FIG. 5-10A). Divide the width into four and put a central rail across. Check the height against the matching parts of the sides, and bevel the top frame member to match the slope of the roof. At the top, let the covering boards project about 3 inches. When you assemble the studio on-site, notch the covering boards for the rafters and trim level with their top surfaces. At the sides, allow the covering to extend by the width of the end uprights. Then when you assemble, the board ends will overlap and you can put a square strip in the corner (FIG. 5-9E).

Make the lower front to match the back width (FIG. 5-10B). The covering boards are level at top and bottom edges, but they extend at the sides in the same way as on the back.

Fully glaze the upper front. Divide it into five glass panels (FIG. 5-11A). The overall length should be the same as the lower front, and the height must match the sloping parts of the sides. All of the parts are rabbeted—5/8 inch deep and 5/8 inch wide should be enough. The outside parts have rabbets on one edge (FIG. 5-11B). The intermediate pieces have rabbets on two edges (FIG. 5-11C). It is possible to dowel parts together, but the best joints are mortise-and-tenon joints (FIG. 5-11D). Treat the corners similar to the intermediate joint shown, but reduce the width of the tenon at the outside. Do not fit the glass until after you have erected the building.

Arrange a sill on the lower front for the upper front to fit over (FIG. 5-11E). You can extend the sill inwards to make a shelf (FIG. 5-11F). It would be difficult to waterproof the joint between the upper frame and the sill with glue. It is better to embed it in jointing compound. Cover the ends of the upper front with strips over the edges of the studio ends, when you assemble it.

Make the opening window in the end the same way as described earlier (FIG. 5-4). Make the door with vertical boards and ledgers and braces (FIG. 5-5). If you do not include a window, put a second brace across. Braces should slope up from the hinged side. Line the doorway and arrange stop strips in the way described earlier for the door you are using.

Make the roof with rafters laid from back to front (FIG. 5-12A). Let the rafters project about 6 inches at back and 12 inches at front. Notch the plywood at the back. At the front, fill the gaps between the rafters with 2-inch-×-3-inch pieces, level with the front of the glazed part (FIG. 5-12B).

Cover the rafters with boards across (FIG. 5-12C) to give a 6-inch overhang at the sides. Thicken all edges with strips underneath. Bevel the front so it is vertical (FIG. 5-12D). Turn the covering material under and nail underneath to the strips. Put battens on top from front to back.

At the front, put a fascia board across (FIG. 5-12E). Do not make it too deep or it will restrict light in the windows. You could give it a decorative shape if you wish.

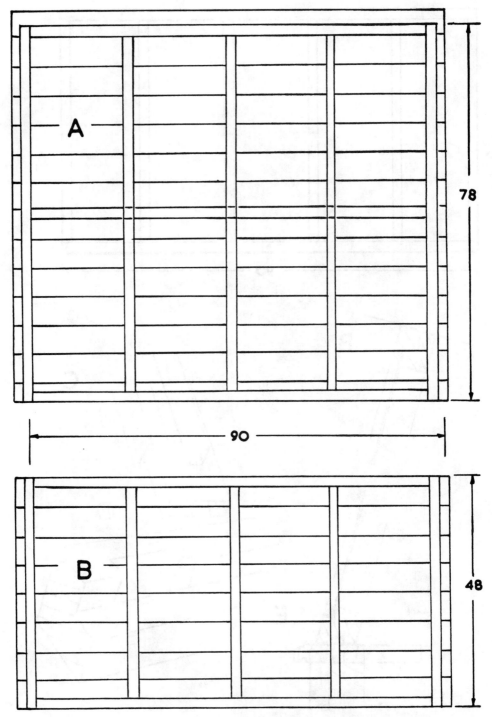

Fig. 5-10. Back and front of the studio.

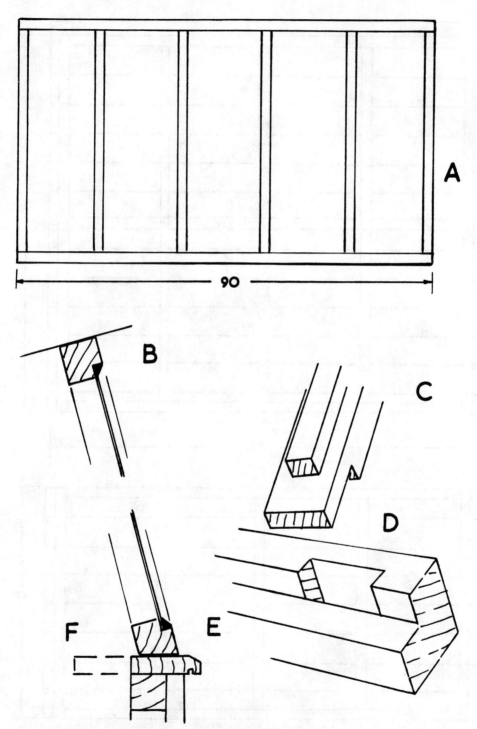

Fig. 5-11. Glazing arrangements for the studio.

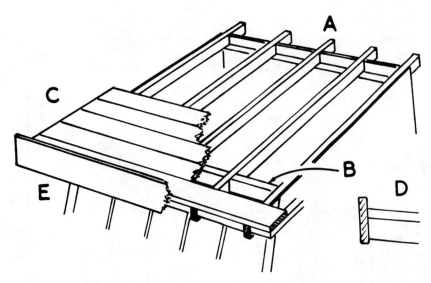

Fig. 5-12. Roof details for the studio.

When you have completed assembly, you can line the walls and under the rafters with plywood or particleboard. If you mounted the building on a concrete base, there could be a wooden floor. Place the boards over the bottom framing parts and lay stiffeners across underneath at about 18-inch intervals. Fit the floor before lining the walls.

Site Shop

If you need to set up a small workshop in one place for a short time, then move it to another site, it has to be strong and easy to disassemble or re-erect. If you might have to leave it on-site unattended, possibly for days, it should be secure. Determined thieves will break into almost anything, but your small shop should resist casual pilferers or vandals.

There are practical limits of size if you are to transport the workshop parts on a truck of moderate size. This site shop (FIG. 5-13) is designed to use two uncut 4-foot-×-8-foot sheets of plywood as roof. This gives a floor area of 78 inches by 84 inches. There is standing head room, and a sectional wooden floor braces the assembly. One window is shown without glass but with a hinged shutter for security.

Construction is with 3/4-inch exterior plywood, which is stronger and more resistant to anyone trying to break in, than any form of boarding. The framing behind it is mainly 2-inch-square strips. Parts are nailed, but it will be an advantage to use waterproof glue between the plywood and framing.

Make the four walls, and temporarily assemble them so the floor parts and roof can be fitted to match. Make the door end first and use this as a guide to

Fig. 5-13. *If you need a shop on-site then want to move it, it can be basic, but must be easy to take down and re-erect.*

sizes of some other parts. Suggested building sizes (FIG. 5-14) can be modified, but remember that they suit single sheets on the roof. Anything larger will complicate the joints there and possibly create bigger wall sections to transport.

Mark out the door end (FIG. 5-15) on two sheets of plywood meeting vertically at the center of the end. Allow for the end wall coming inside the side wall plywood when assembled (FIG. 5-15A). You could cut joints between the framing parts, but there is considerable strength in the plywood, and it should be sufficient to merely butt framing parts to each other and secure them with glue and nails. Cut the door opening, and glue and nail the sheets closely on the vertical strip above the doorway.

Make the opposite end to the same outline. Because there is no door, you can continue the framing both ways across (FIG. 5-15B). Drill the corner uprights of both ends for 3/8-inch bolts at about 18-inch intervals. When you make the first

Materials List for Site Shop

9 end uprights	2	× 2	×	96
4 end rails	2	× 2	×	78
1 end upright	2	× 2	×	24
4 end rafters	2	× 2	×	48
5 side uprights	2	× 2	×	80
3 side uprights	2	× 2	×	42
4 floor framing	2	× 2	×	80
10 floor framing	2	× 2	×	44
2 roof frames	2	× 3	×	84
2 roof frames	2	× 2	×	84
10 roof frames	2	× 2	×	48
2 roof edges	3/4	× 1 1/2	×	98
4 roof edges	3/4	× 1 1/2	×	50
2 shutter frames	1	× 2	×	30
3 shutter frames	1	× 2	×	26
2 window frames	1	× 3	×	32
2 window frames	1	× 3	×	28
2 door linings	1	× 3	×	80
1 door lining	1	× 3	×	32
2 door frames	2	× 2	×	76
4 door frames	2	× 2	×	30

All covering 3/4 exterior plywood

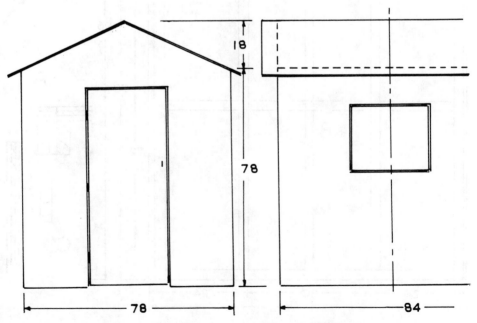

Fig. 5-14. Main sizes of the site shop.

assembly, use these holes as drill guides to make matching holes in the adjoining uprights.

When you make the front (FIG. 5-16A), allow for the plywood extending enough to cover the edges of the front and back assemblies (FIG. 5-15C). Arrange for the sheets to meet with a vertical joint over the central upright. Cut out and frame the window opening with uprights (FIG. 5-16B).

Make the height to match the end assemblies, but bevel the top rail to suit the roof angle (FIG. 5-16C).

Make the back in a similar way, but leave out the window uprights and continue the central upright/joint cover all the way (FIG. 5-16D).

Assemble the four walls temporarily on a level surface, and check squareness. Cut plywood floor panels to meet centrally across the shop (FIG. 5-16E). Arrange them to rest on the bottom rails of the walls. Notch them to fit at corners. Don't aim for a precise fit, or you could have difficulty when assembling on some sites. Clearances should be between $1/4$ inch and $1/2$ inch.

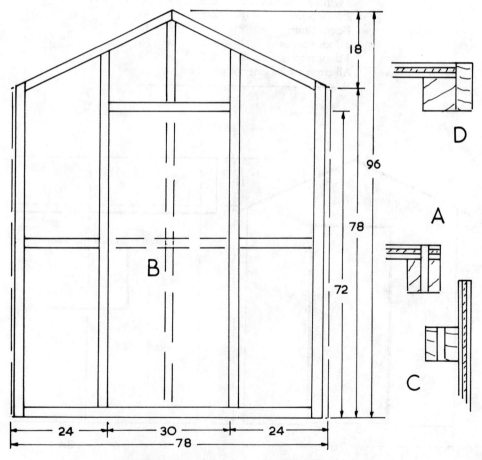

Fig. 5-15. Details of the ends of the site shop.

Put sufficient framing below the floor sections to resist bending under expected loads. Frame to fit easily inside the wall rails (FIG. 5-16F) and at the meeting edges, then put others across (FIG. 5-16G).

With the floor holding the building in shape, try roof panels in turn. Allow for the plywood meeting closely along the ridge and with even overhangs at the edges (FIG. 5-17A). Frame the outer edges with strips to provide stiffness and fastening places for turned-in roof covering (FIG. 5-17B). Make other framing to pro-

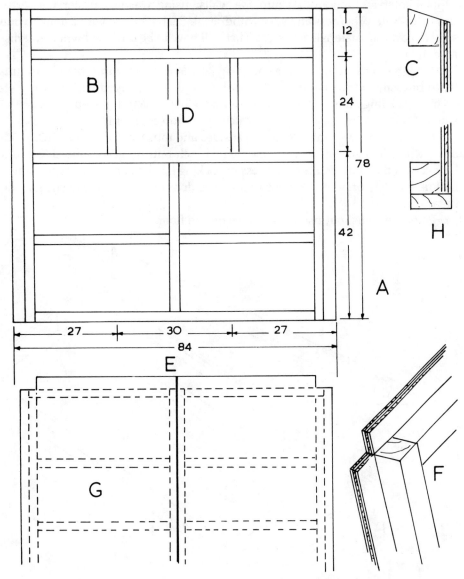

Fig. 5-16. *Details of sides and floor of the site shop.*

vide stiffness and to locate the roof panel by fitting loosely inside the walls. The strips (FIG. 5-17C) need not meet closely at corners. For stiffness along the otherwise unsupported ridge, use 2-inch-×-3-inch wood, beveled to suit (FIG. 5-17D).

When the two roof sections are put in position, they should rest against each other along the ridge, and the locating strips inside should hold them in place, with not more than 1/2-inch tolerance. You could paint the roof sections, but it would be better to cover them individually with tarred felt or other material. Turn it in and nail it all round. When you assemble on site, drive screws at about 12-inch intervals downwards into the walls, using washers under the screw heads for waterproofness and easy withdrawal. Seal the ridge with a 6-inch-wide strip of covering material tacked on. That will have to be scrapped when you disassemble.

Line the edges of the window opening (FIG. 5-16H) all around. Make the shutter to fit easily in the opening (FIG. 5-18A) with plywood edged with 1-inch-×-2-inch strips. Hinge the shutter at the lower edge (FIG. 5-18B). Put stop strips on the sides of the opening, and arrange a catch at the top center inside.

Line the door opening (FIG. 5-15D) at sides and top. Make the door (FIG. 5-18C) of plywood framed with strips. Use three 4-inch butt hinges at one side and a lock at the other side. For compactness in packing for transport, you might omit a handle and rely only on a key for pulling the door open. Put a stop strip inside the frame.

Paint the walls, but use preservative on the floor.

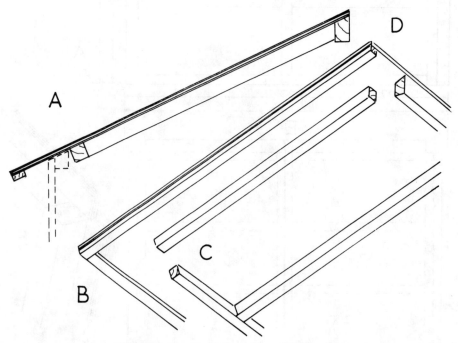

Fig. 5-17. Details of the roof on the site shop.

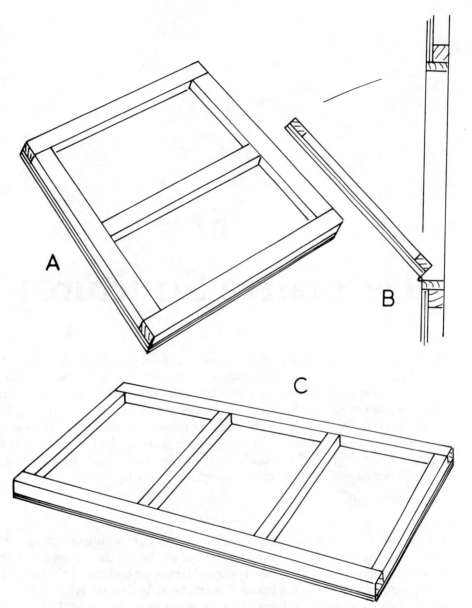

Fig. 5-18. *Shutter and door for the site shop.*

6

Decorative Structures

Most small buildings will have practical uses, and they might be decorative to a limited extent, but there are others where decoration is a first consideration. It could be a complete building or it could be a semi-open structure. The structure might be there to support foliage that provides the decoration.

If the support of foliage is the main purpose, you should make sure the structure is strong and durable, as repairs after years of plant growth have covered the wood might be impossible to make. Be careful that any preservative used will not have an adverse effect on anything growing nearby.

Gazebo

You can use a building with a sheltered porch for sunbathing or sitting out in chairs even when the weather is not perfect, since the structure provides shelter from wind and rain. It can provide a peaceful retreat for anyone who wants to get away from activities inside the house. It might be a place for studying. It could be a play center for children, although it is not primarily a playhouse. The enclosed part of the building will provide full shelter when you need it, and it makes a place to store chairs, tables, games, equipment, or gardening tools.

The gazebo shown in FIG. 6-1 has a base that is 9 feet square, divided in half by a partition with a door and windows (FIG. 6-2). The upper part is open, with sheltering lower sides and a rail front. The door is arranged to lift off so you can put it inside, instead of it swinging and interfering with seating on the porch. The exterior probably will look best with shiplap siding, and you could use that on the partition. You could, however, cover all the building or just the partition

Materials List for Gazebo

Floor

7 joists	2	×	3	×	110
14 boards	1	×	6	×	110
	or	equivalent			
2 ends	1	×	3	×	110

Partition and back

6 uprights	2	×	2	×	88
2 uprights	2	×	2	×	24
4 window uprights	2	×	2	×	32
5 rails	2	×	2	×	110
4 rails	2	×	2	×	36
4 tops	2	×	2	×	60

Sides

8 uprights	2	×	2	×	88
2 uprights	2	×	2	×	40
4 rails	2	×	2	×	110
2 top tails	2	×	2 or 3	×	120

Front

1 rail	2	×	2	×	110
2 rails	2	×	2	×	60
3 uprights	2	×	2	×	24
4 uprights	2	×	2	×	42
4 rails	2	×	2	×	28
4 posts	1¼	×	1¼	×	42
2 post supports	2	×	2	×	24
2 rail tops	1¼	×	3	×	28

Edge covers

2 side-edge tops	1¼	×	4	×	54
2 side uprights	1	×	4	×	70
2 window sides	1	×	7	×	30
2 window sides	1	×	5	×	30
2 corner fillers	1	×	1	×	88

Windows

8 surrounds	1	×	4	×	28
8 stops	1	×	1	×	28
8 frames	2	×	2	×	28

Door

6 boards	1	×	6	×	80
	or equivalent				
3 ledgers	1	×	6	×	36
2 braces	1	×	6	×	36
2 pegs	1½	×	1½	×	12

Roof

32 boards		×	6	×	60
	or equivalent				
2 battens	1	×	3	×	108
2 edges	2	×	1¼	×	120
4 ends	1¼	×	1¼	×	60
2 edge decorations	1	×	3	×	120
4 bargeboards	1	×	6	×	66
8 battens	¼	×	1	×	60

Cladding

1- × -6 shiplap boards or equivalent

and door with plywood. The gazebo is built on a floor, which forms part of the assembly.

Most of the framing can be 2-inch-square wood, although you could increase that to 2-inch-×-3-inch wood for greater strength. The roof is boarded, without separate purlins, and is covered in the usual way. Much of the decorative appearance comes from the bargeboards and matching eaves strips. The fence at the front has square uprights, but if you have the use of a lathe, they would look attractive if made them as turned spindles with square ends.

Start with the floor, which should be 9 feet square. Use 1-inch boards and 2-inch-×-3-inch joists at about 18-inch centers (FIG. 6-3A). Close the joists' ends with strips across (FIG. 6-3B).

Fig. 6-1. *This gazebo has a sheltered porch and ample inside accommodations.*

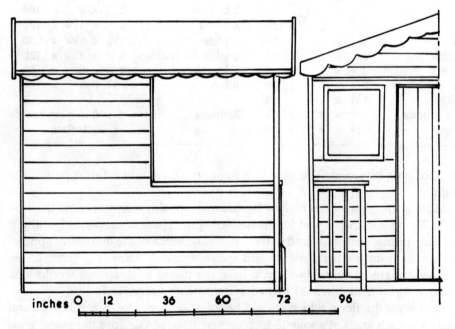

inches 0   12   36   60   72   96

Fig. 6-2. *Two views of the gazebo of the suggested size.*

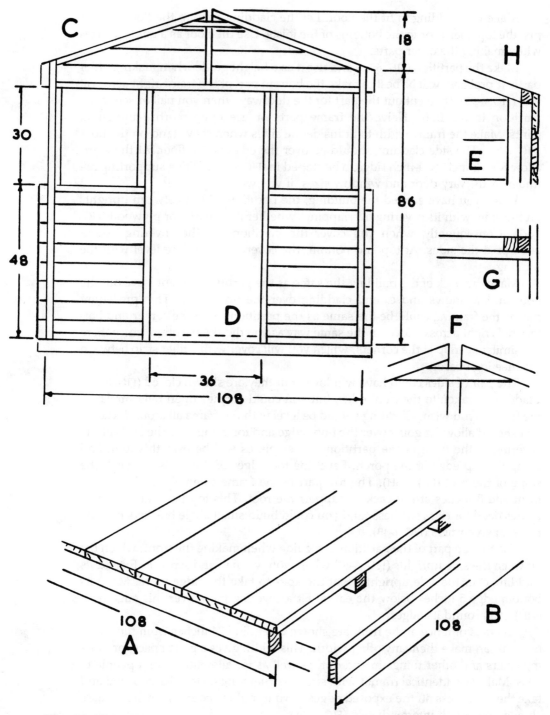

Fig. 6-3. *The gazebo floor (A,B), its front (C,D) and constructional details (E,F,G,H).*

Make the building to fit the floor. Let the cladding overlap the floor—either just the top boards or to the bottoms of the joists. Use the floor as a guide to sizes when making the other parts.

Make the partition (FIG. 6-3C) and use it as a height guide when making other parts. It probably will be best to make the bottom part of the frame right across at first (FIG. 6-3D), then cut out the part for the doorway when you nail or screw the partition to the floor. Halve the frame parts or use open mortise-and-tenon joints. Make the frame width to fit inside the sides when they stand on the floor (FIG. 6-3E). The side cladding should go over the edge of the floor. At the apex, allow for a 2-inch-×-4-inch ridge to be slotted in (FIG. 6-3F), with a supporting rail underneath. Vary door and window sizes, if you wish.

When you have erected the building, the partition will fit between uprights on the side, with its covering overlapping, whether it is boards or plywood (FIG. 6-3G). Consequently, when you cover the partition, let the covering extend enough at the sides. At top and bottom, the covering should be level with the framing.

Make the back of the building the same as the partition, except leave out the door and windows and extend cladding over the floor edge. This procedure means the framing could be the same as the partition, with the center and bottom rails right across. Cover in the same way as you did the partition, since there is a similar overlap at the corners, which you will cover with a filler strip between the meeting boards.

The pair of sides could have windows, but they are shown closed (FIG. 6-4A). Cladding is taken to the front edge, but you could arrange open rails similar to the front, if you wish. Cladding should be level with the frame all around, except you should allow for going over the floor edge and for going over the ends of the covering at the front of the partition. Cover pieces will be over this joint and along the top edge of the porch. Bevel the top edges of the sides to match the slope of the roof (FIG. 6-3H). The top part of the frame extends 6 inches at the front and 3 inches at the back to support the roof. This top part can also be 3 inches deep for extra stiffness, and you could build small angle brackets into the front, open corners (FIG. 6-4B).

Use the top part of the partition as a guide when making the front, which fits between the side uprights (FIG. 6-4C) where you will nail and screw it. Extend its cladding over the side uprights. Slot the apex to take the ridge piece. Make its bottom edge 5 inches below the eaves. Fit a covering piece over this edge (FIG. 6-4D) and around its edges.

The rails or fence at the front are shown extending 24 inches from the sides, but you can make them any other width. This width gives a good space for moving chairs and other things in and out, as well as for allowing several people to pass. Make two identical frames with strong corner joints. Use planed wood and take the sharpness off the exposed edges. Two uprights about $1^{1}/_{2}$ inches square should be enough intermediately (FIG. 6-5A).

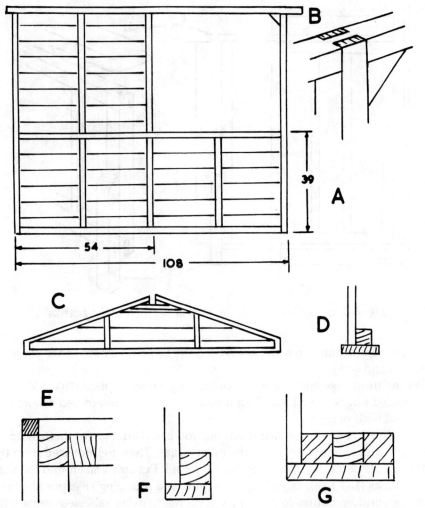

Fig. 6-4. A side of the gazebo (A,B), a roof truss (C), and assembly details (D,E,F,G)

You will mount this assembly on the edge of the floor and you should securely screw or bolt it to the floor and the side uprights. Arrange an overlapping piece to extend to the bottom of the floor (FIG. 6-5B) to stiffen the post at the open end of each piece.

Start erection of the building by bolting the two sides to the back and the partition—3/8-inch coach bolts at about 24-inch intervals should be sufficient. Square this assembly on the floor, and nail the bottom edges down. Cut out the bottom piece across the doorway. Put square filler pieces in the rear corners (FIG. 6-4E). Cover exposed cladding edges at the partition and front (FIG. 6-4F). Put strips on

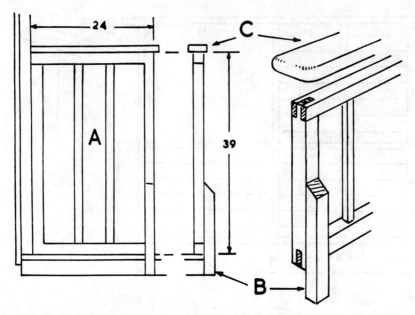

Fig. 6-5. Sizes and details of the fence at the front of the gazebo.

each side of the window frames so they are the same thickness as the cladding (FIGS. 6-4G and 6-6A).

Fix the front rails and make an overlapping covering piece (FIG. 6-5C) with well rounded edges. It will look best if you fix it with counterbored screws and cover them with plugs.

The two windows are shown fixed, but you could arrange for them to open, either with hinges at the top or on the outer edges. They are protected from the weather by the porch, so there is no need for a sill. Put strips all around the window openings (FIG. 6-6B), extending out a little, and rounding all exposed edges. Make the window frames to fit closely (FIG. 6-6C), using rabbeted strips (FIG. 6-6D). You could screw the strips directly in place, but it will probably be easier to make a good, weathertight fit with stop strips inside (FIG. 6-6E). Fit the glass with putty after you paint the woodwork.

Line the sides and top of the doorway in the same way as the window openings. Put stop pieces near the inner edges (FIG. 6-7A). Make the door (FIG. 6-7B) an easy fit in the opening. Have the edge of the bottom ledger about 2 inches from the bottom of the door. If the top ledger has only a small clearance below the top stop strip in the opening, you can fit a lock with a keyhole there or arrange a catch that turns with a knob. Place the other ledger centrally and arrange braces both ways.

At the bottom, fit two pegs to go into holes in the floor (FIG. 6-7C). Notch over the bottom ledger and taper the extending ends slightly (FIG. 6-7D). Glue and screw these a few inches in from the sides of the door. Mark holes in the floor

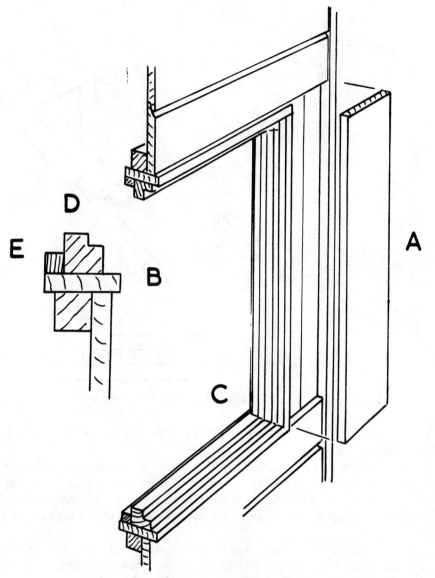

Fig. 6-6. *Window construction for the gazebo.*

where you can drop the pegs in while you angle the door forward so they hold it fairly close to the stop strips. When the top of the door is held with a lock or catch, the building will be secured.

Fit the ridge to extend 6 inches at the front and 3 inches at the back. If necessary, trim the ends of the eaves strips to the same length (FIG. 6-8A,B). You can board the roof direct, using 1-inch-×-6-inch boards, preferably tongue-and-groove. If you use boards with plain edges, there can be a central batten (FIG.

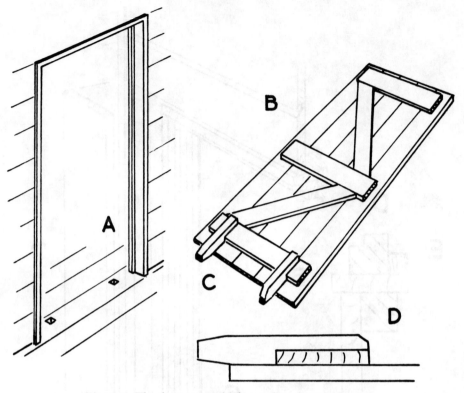

Fig. 6-7. The doorway and lift-out door for the gazebo.

6-8C) to prevent the boards from warping out of line. You do not need to fix the batten to the back or partition.

Nail the boards to the ridge and to the eaves, where they should extend about 4 inches (FIG. 6-8D). At the eaves, put a strip underneath, with its edge and the ends of the boards cut vertically, if you are adding the side decoration (FIG. 6-8E). Put similar square-edge strips down the end boards (FIG. 6-8F) to support the bargeboards.

Carry roof covering over from eaves to eaves and turn under for nailing. Turn under at the ends. Allow ample overlap where there are any joints, and make joints in the direction that will let water run away from them. You could add capping strips, but they probably will not be necessary on this small roof. Nail battens down the slope at each side at about 18-inch intervals.

If the decoration on the lower edges of the bargeboards and eaves boards is to look right, the curves should be uniform. Make a template of at least two curves, using scrap plywood or hardboard (FIG. 6-8G). Use this template to mark all the shaped edges and to check them after shaping. Nail the boards to the roof to complete construction.

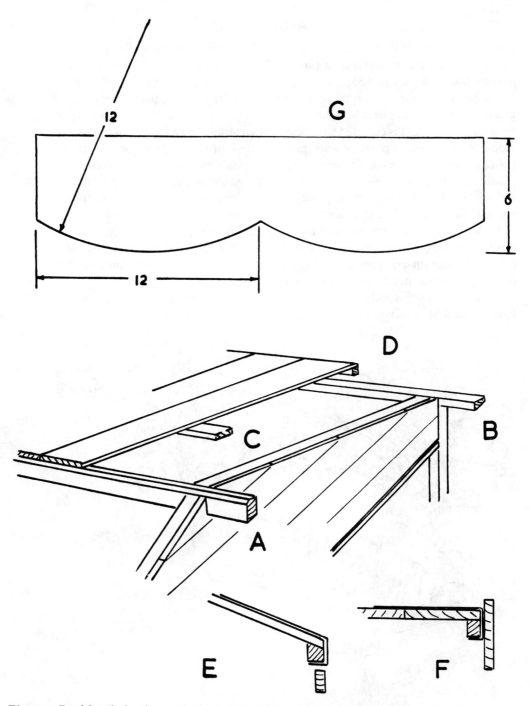

Fig. 6-8. *Roof details for the gazebo (A, B, C, D, E, F) and a template for marking edge decorations.*

Arbor

If you make a pergola structure with a seat, it becomes an arbor. Foliage grows over and around it and makes it a shelter. The foliage may be quite dense, except at the front, or it may just form a roof. Roses particularly are associated with an arbor, but you can use any type of climbing plant. You could build a pergola and place a seat under it, but it is better to build the seat in. Because this is a permanent structure and it is exposed to all kinds of weather, you must make the seat of wood. Any softening must be with portable cushions. This fact does not mean the seat cannot be at a comfortable angle for use without cushions on occasions.

The arbor shown in FIG. 6-9 has inverted V legs supporting a flat top similar to a pergola. At each end, a strut parallel with a leg slopes up to give additional support to the top. This strut sets the angle of the seat-back, which has vertical slats. You can make the bottom of the seat solid or slatted. The legs go into the ground, and crosspieces prevent them from sinking too far. The suggested sizes (FIG. 6-10A) are for an arbor 6 feet high and about 7 feet long, but you can alter these to suit your needs or available space.

You can use softwood treated with preservative or a more durable hardwood. Remember that once you erect the arbor and foliage is growing over it, you can-

Fig. 6-9. Make an arborlike pergola so foliage can form a roof over a seat.

Materials List for Arbor

4 legs	2 × 4 × 84
2 struts	2 × 3 × 70
2 tops	2 × 4 × 74
2 bottoms	2 × 3 × 66
2 seat supports	2 × 4 × 48
6 beams	2 × 4 × 120
4 seat rails	2 × 2 × 84
2 seat dividers	2 × 2 × 20
12 seat slats	1 × 4 × 20
2 seat boards	1 × 6 × 84 or slats
4 platform strips	1 × 4 × 74
6 platform supports	2 × 2 × 22

not do much to treat or repair it. Its original construction must be strong enough to have an expected life of many years. Bolts ought to be galvanized to minimize rust. Any glue should be a waterproof type, and screws should be plated or made of a noncorrosive metal. The main parts are 2 inch × 3 inch or a 4-inch section.

Start by setting out an end. If you want to set tools, the angles are 15 degrees. From the ground line, draw a centerline square to it; then 72 inches up, mark the apex of a triangle with a 39-inch spread at the base (FIG. 6-11A). Draw the top across (FIG. 6-11B), and mark the widths of the wood. Draw the seat support across the legs (FIG. 6-11C). The seat top is symmetrical about the centerline of this seat support and the strut slopes up from the back of it, parallel with the front leg (FIG. 6-11D). This layout gives you all the shapes and sizes you need to start construction.

Notch the tops to take the lengthwise beams (FIG. 6-11E). Let the legs meet on the beam and drill through for bolts. Spread the bottoms and secure them with the ground strips (FIG. 6-11F). On this framework, mark where the seat bearers come. Put these pieces across and add the long struts (FIG. 6-11G), marking where they cross and where you want to drill for bolts or cut joints.

On the seat bearers, mark and cut the notches for the lengthwise seat supports, not more than 1¹/₂ inches deep (FIG. 6-11H). The strut joins by halving. This halving is best cut with a dovetail shape (FIG. 6-11J). Cut the notches to take the lengthwise back supports (FIG. 6-11K). At the top, halve the strut into the top piece. Assemble the pair of ends, with bolts where parts overlap and glue and screws at the joints.

The seat back has vertical slats with a curve cut on their top edge (FIG. 6-10B). You might prefer some other shape. Make the two 2-inch-square rails, notching ends to fit the notches in the struts. Have the back slats too long at first. Fit them temporarily to the rails. Bend a batten over them and draw a curve on their tops. Remove the slats to cut their curved tops and round all exposed edges. Glue and screw them in place.

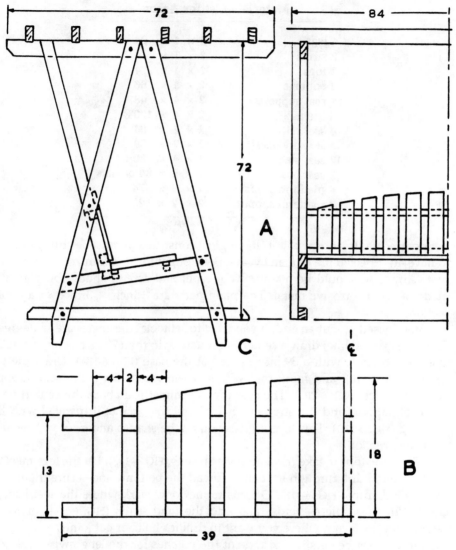

Fig. 6-10. Sizes of the arbor.

Make the seat supports to the same length as the back supports. Put pieces between them—if you divide the length into three, that should be sufficient (FIG. 6-12A). The seat top could be solid and made up of any boards of convenient width (FIG. 6-12B), or you could use slats with gaps between them (FIG. 6-12C). In any case, round the front and top edges. Glue and screw the seat parts together.

Glue and screw the seat rails into the end assemblies. With the aid of the top beams, the seat rails provide lengthwise rigidity to the structure. Check squareness, both upright and front-to-back. Because of handling problems due to

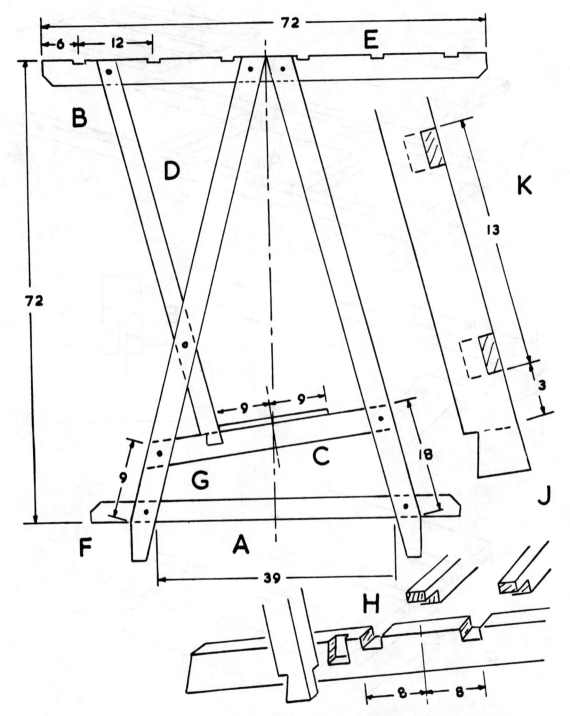

Fig. 6-11. Detail of one end of the arbor.

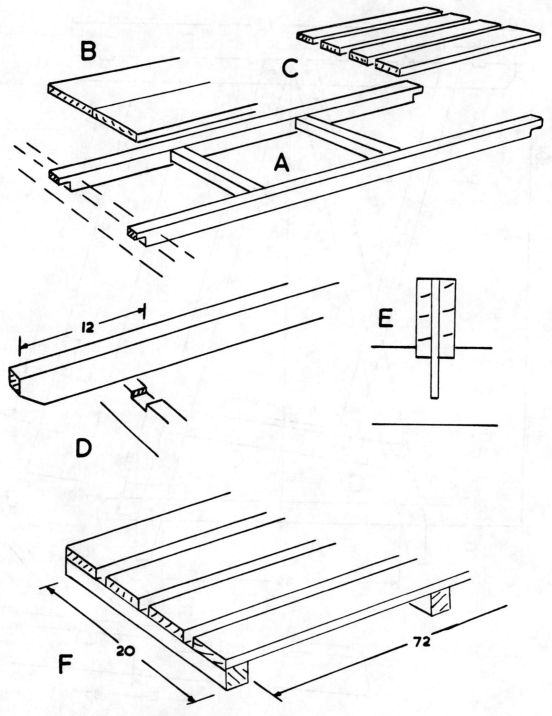

B

C

A

12

E

D

F

20

72

Fig. 6-12. Construction of parts of the arbor.

weight, it probably will be advisable to erect the arbor in position before fitting the beams. The legs are shown with short points to push into the ground in FIG. 6-10C. If this design does not suit your situation, you could set the legs in concrete, or you might want to bury flat boards under the legs in loose soil. If the ground is not level, you might have to sink the boards by different amounts. Check with a level on the bottom crosspieces and on the seat or on a board between the bottom parts.

Make the top beams all identical. They should overhang by 12 inches or more on the ends (FIG. 6-12D). Bevel the undersides of the ends. Drill down through for a 1/2-inch steel rod to be driven in to act as a dowel at each crossing (FIG. 6-12E). To prevent the entry of water and the start of rot and rust, you could drive the rod below the surface and fill the hole with a wooden plug or mastic, or nail a thin piece of wood above it.

So plants will grow and engulf the arbor, there should be as much soil area around the base as possible, but you might want to lay a concrete slab in front of the seat to provide a clean, dry area for the feet. More in keeping with the arbor would be a platform of slats on crosspieces (FIG. 6-12F). Make it as a unit, so you can lift it occasionally.

If you paint or treat with preservative after you have erected the arbor, do it long before plants start to climb, so solvents will evaporate before the shoots come into contact with the structure. As plants climb, you might have to encourage them to go where you want by tying them to nails or by providing temporary strips of wood across the uprights. Ideally, you should have the arbor in position well before the start of the growing season, then you can watch progress, although it will be a few years before the foliage densely covers the roof and walls of your arbor.

Gateway

Something more than just a simple gate in the fence will provide character to your yard or garden and improve its appearance. It could be an access from the road on your boundary or between parts of the garden—opening up a new vista as you go from the vegetable plot to a flower garden. A gateway that has depth as well as width helps in maintaining privacy. Such a gateway is best made with a roof, which can improve the looks of the structure and offer shelter from sudden storms or excessive sunshine.

This gateway (FIG. 6-13) is a roofed shelter with picket-fence sides and a gate to match. You could alter the design to fit in with an existing boundary or dividing fence. With vines and other plants around and over it, it becomes a sort of arbor. You could build it with an open-topped roof if all you need is a framework for climbing vines.

The suggested sizes (FIG. 6-14) are for a gateway 5 feet square at the base, with an overall height of 8 feet and head room of 6 feet, 6 inches underneath. You might wish to adapt sizes to suit your needs. At the suggested size, the roof pro-

Fig. 6-13. A roofed gateway is attractive and gives shelter and privacy.

Materials List for Gateway

4 posts	4	×	4	×	108	
4 rafters	2	×	4	×	48	
4 purlins	2	×	3	×	64	
1 ridge	2	×	3	×	64	
4 bargeboards	1	×	6	×	48	
1 tie	2	×	4	×	54	
2 roof panels	44	×	64	×	¹/₂	plywood
2 roof edges	³/₄	×	1¹/₂	×	64	
4 side rails	2	×	4	×	60	
2 gate rails	2	×	4	×	54	
30 pickets	1	×	4	×	36	
1 gate brace	2	×	4	×	66	

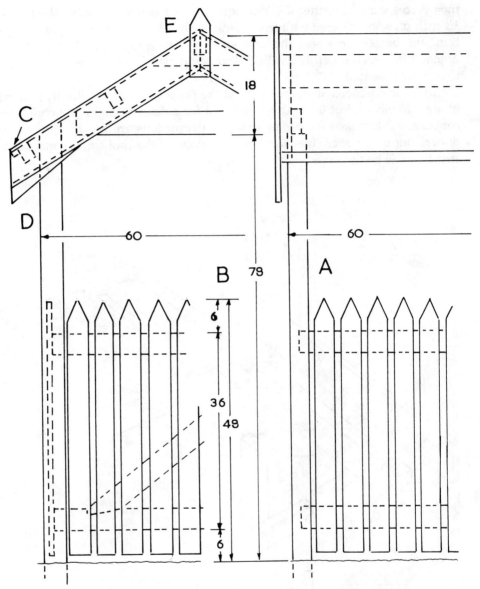

Fig. 6-14. Suggested sizes for the gateway.

vides plenty of shelter. You could reduce the back-to-front size to 2 feet or less, if all you want is an arch. However, with a square ground plan, the gate can be made to swing inwards and fasten against a side, without anything projecting when you want a clear run through.

The parts are mostly stock sections and could be hardwood or softwood. Treating with preservative is advisable. The posts could be made from 2-inch- × -4-

inch pieces joined together if 4-inch-square wood is not available. The roof is 1/2-inch plywood covered with felt or other material. Besides serving as decoration, the bargeboards seal the roof ends and its supports. Most parts are notched into each other and nailed. You could also use waterproof glue, but that is not essential.

In the instructions, it is assumed that the posts will be sunk directly into the ground 18 inches, but in weak ground and for greater strength you could use concrete, as described for earlier projects. Instructions are for the gateway as drawn, but if you alter sizes and keep the slope of the roof similar, main construction will be the same.

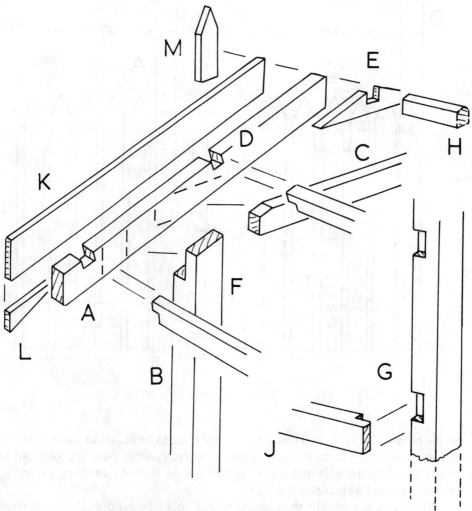

Fig. 6-15. Constructional details of the gateway.

The key parts, which control the sizes of many other parts, are the two pairs of rafters (FIGS. 6-15A and 6-16A). Set out the slope (FIG. 6-16B) full size. Mark a rafter to this angle. At the apex, it is cut vertically (FIG. 6-16C). At the eaves, make it extend enough to take a purlin and the overhang of the roof (FIG. 6-16D). Mark the position of another purlin (FIG. 6-16E).

Draw on the positions of the posts (FIGS. 6-15B and 6-16F) and the tie (FIGS. 6-15C and 6-16G). Notch for the purlins half their depths (FIG. 6-15D). Cut the two pairs of rafters to match.

Assemble each pair of rafters together. Use a 1-inch-thick piece at the apex (FIG. 6-15E), notched to take the ridge piece. Put the tie across. Although all other parts can be nailed, this is best bolted because it has to resist any tendency for the assembly to spread. Two $1/2$-inch bolts at each end would be suitable. Check the width across the marked positions of the posts.

Cut the two pairs of posts to size (FIG. 6-14A). Bevel and notch each top to take its rafter (FIG. 6-15F). Allow for the amount a post will go into the ground, and mark the positions of the fence rails (FIG. 6-14B). The rails could be notched right through, but you can avoid their ends showing with shorter notches (FIG. 6-15G).

Dig oversize holes for the bottoms of the posts so you can move them to get them plumb and correctly located during assembly. Join the posts to their rafters, so you have two end assemblies ready to erect. Cut at least two purlins to length. Stand the end assemblies in their holes and put a purlin across at each side. Check squareness and that the posts are upright. Stand back and look at the gateway from several angles to see that it looks right. Tamp some earth loosely into the holes to prevent movement. Fit all purlins. Make the ridge (FIG. 6-15H) to fit into the end supports. Bevel its top edge to match the slope of the roof.

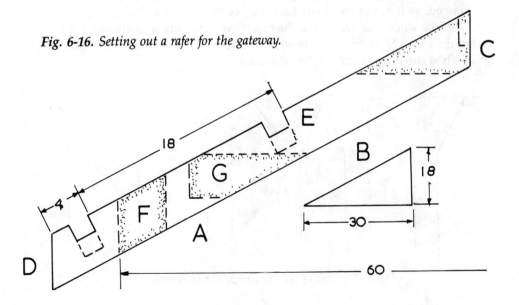

Fig. 6-16. Setting out a rafter for the gateway.

Your assembly should now be reasonably rigid, but it will help to nail on the roof plywood. Thicken underneath at the eaves (FIG. 6-14C) to give a strong edge for tacking the covering felt. Cut the plywood level at the outside edges of the rafters.

Make a final check of squareness, then fit the fence rails (FIG. 6-15J) to hold the posts, and tamp down the earth around the bottoms of the posts.

Cover the roof with felt or other material, taken across from eaves to eaves, turned under each side, and nailed down onto the rafters at the ends. Cut barge-boards (FIG. 6-15K). They meet at the top, but should extend about 1/2 inch at the eaves and be arranged to come equally above and below the roof ends. You could leave these as plain parallel boards, but they are shown with tapered pieces added (FIGS. 6-14D and 6-15L) and with finials at the ridge (FIGS. 6-14E and 6-15M). Plain strips are shown, but you could turn pieces for a different effect. Nail on the bargeboards closely to limit the amount of rainwater running into the joints.

The picket pieces for the fence and gate are the same. You can use your own ideas for the treatment of tops. Some possible shapes are suggested (FIG. 6-17). Any points should not be taken to an acute angle, but should be square across or rounded. If you choose hollowed sides, you can drill half-holes with a Forstner bit or hold rails against each other to drill with an ordinary bit.

On gate and fences, allow for 4-inch strips about 1 inch apart, but adjust them in the available spaces to give even gaps. Nail the pickets to the fence rails, so their bottom edges are clear of the ground by about 1 inch.

Cut the gate rails (FIG. 6-18A) to fit between the posts with 1/2-inch clearance. Cut all the gate pickets to size and shape. Mark on them where the rails will come. Allow ample clearance at ground level. Put the pickets on a flat floor with the rails in position over them. Check squareness by comparing diagonal measurements. Arrange the diagonal brace to slope upwards from the side that will be hinged, as it has to resist any tendency of the gate to sag.

Put the wood that will make the brace over the rails so it crosses 3 inches in from the ends. Mark on the rails where this comes. Notch the rails (FIG. 6-18B)—3/4 inch at the deep point will be satisfactory.

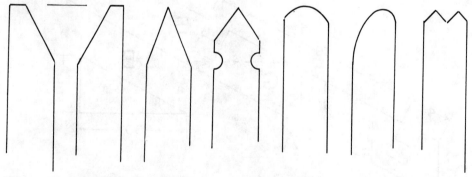

Fig. 6-17. Tops of palings can be cut in several ways.

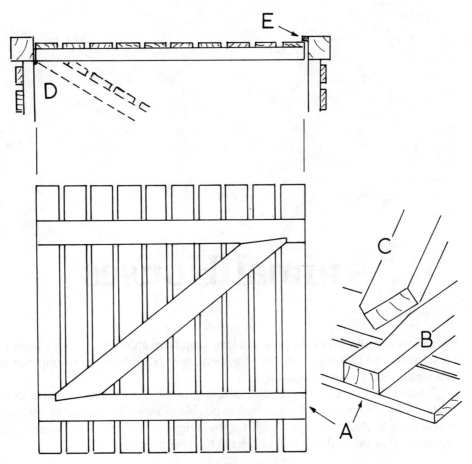

Fig. 6-18. Design for a gate.

Nail the outer pickets to the rails. Try the gate in closed and open positions between the posts. Again check squareness, then nail on all pickets securely. Mark the ends of the brace from the rail notches (FIG. 6-18C). Cut the brace so its ends are a tight fit. Nail it in and the pickets to it.

Hinge the gate with its rails level with the inner surface of a post (FIG. 6-18D). You could use 4-inch butt or T hinges. At the other post put a stop piece the full depth of the gate (FIG. 6-18E). Arrange a catch to hold the gate closed. If this is at the top rail level, you can reach over to operate it. The gate will swing inwards to rest against the side fence. It might be sufficient for it to just rest there, or you could provide a hook or catch to stop the gate swinging closed unintentionally.

7

Animal Houses

If you have pets, breed birds, raise poultry, keep farm animals, or own a pony or horse, you need housing or shelters for them, which might be very simple or as substantial as many other buildings.

Smaller shelters can be prefabricated, but many animal shelters have to be built on-site. For some stock, you need to be able to move the shelter by carrying or wheeling it. Build strong enough for the animals involved to be housed, but remember that the building will also have to resist predators.

Mini Hen House

If you want to keep just a few laying hens, you do not need a large house for them. This poultry house is intended for four hens or maybe six bantams. You could use it for ducks, but you would have to fit it with a solid floor instead of the slats. The mini hen house shown in FIGS. 7-1 and 7-2 is without a run, but if you want to stop your little flock from wandering too far, you can make a frame with wire netting.

Construction may be quite light, and a skin of plywood on 1-inch-×-2-inch strips is suggested. There is a pop hole with a sliding door. One perch is provided, and there is a single nest box opposite it. The roof hinges open for access to the entire house, which you can move easily to a different position.

Make the front (FIG. 7-2A) with the framing having its 2-inch side against the plywood for top and sides, but having the 1-inch side towards the plywood across the bottom. The hole is 11 inches wide and high.

Make the door and its guides with rabbets to clear the pop hole. Frame the

Fig. 7-1. A mini hen house made of plywood and suitable for a few laying hens.

Materials List for Mini Hen House

7 pieces	1 × 2 × 38
6 pieces	1 × 2 × 44
6 pieces	1 × 2 × 32
4 pieces	1 × 2 × 26
1 perch	1 × 1 × 44
9 slats	1 × 1 × 38
2 sides	30- × -42- × -⅜ plywood
1 front	30- × -38- × -⅜ plywood
1 back	26- × -38- × -⅜ plywood
1 roof	42- × -50- × -⅜ plywood
Nest box and door	12- × -36- × -⅜ plywood

back in the same way as the front, but make it 24 inches high. Drill 2-inch ventilation holes high in each part.

Make the pair of sides (FIG. 7-2B). Use the framing strips in the same manner as the back and front, but at the corners, allow for the plywood to overlap (FIG. 7-2C). Bevel the top edge of the front to match the slope of the sides. There is no need to bevel the top edge of the back. Notch the corner strips over each other at the bottom, when you nail the walls together.

The roof is a single piece of plywood overhanging 3 inches all around (FIG. 7-2D). Frame around the underside to fit very loosely inside the walls—this prevents roof warping since you do not make a close fit in the walls. At the front,

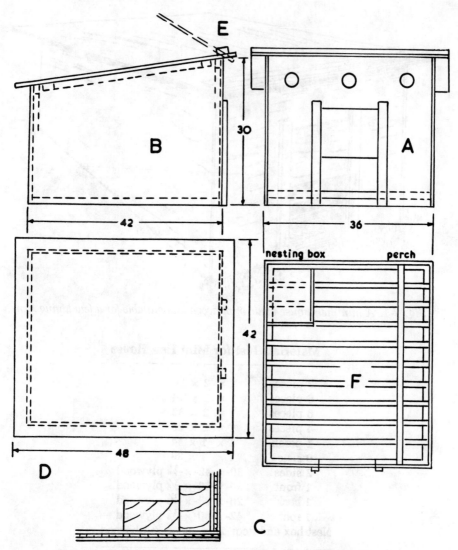

Fig. 7-2. Sizes and internal arrangements of the mini hen house.

where you are to place the hinges, put a strip across above the plywood (FIG. 7-2E) to take the screws. Two 3-inch hinges should be adequate. You could have a fastener at the back, but its weight will hold the roof closed.

Put supports for the perch (FIG. 7-3A) at both ends, about 6 inches from the bottom and side. The perch is a square section, but take sharpness off the edges.

Make the slatted floor (FIG. 7-2F) of 1-inch-square strips with rounded edges, nailing them 3 inches apart (FIG. 7-3B) to the bottom strips on the sides. If the

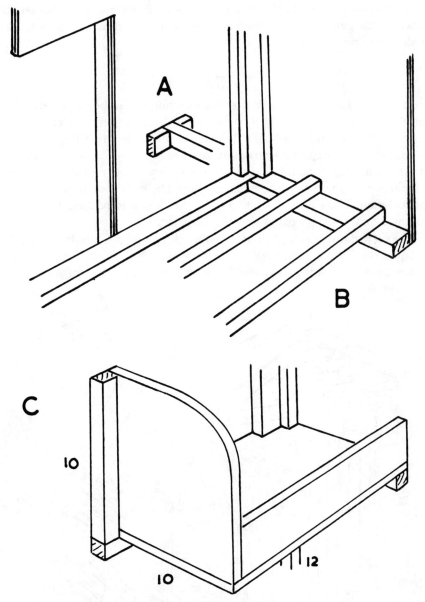

Fig. 7-3. Perches and laying box for the hen house.

house is for ducks, put in a plywood floor in place of the slats, or on top of the slats if you might want to use the house for hens later.

Make the nesting box of plywood, with framing strips holding it into the corner (FIG. 7-3C). The sizes shown should suit one bird, but check your bird's needs. The only access to the nesting box is by lifting the roof. No feeding or drinking arrangements are in the house, since it is assumed it is only to be used for sleeping and nesting.

Barn

If you need to house larger animals, the building has to be bigger and stronger than those described so far in this chapter. A horse or other large animal (or a group of animals) might put considerable strain on the structure, so it has to be substantial. You need a good barrier inside to spread any load on the walls. If the barrier is a strong, smooth lining, that reduces any risk of damage to the animals and makes cleaning easier. The building should be high enough to allow for good air circulation. These facts mean that if the building is to be adequate for its purpose, you have to be prepared to build fairly large.

The barn shown in FIG. 7-4 has a double-slope roof and double doors. It is 11 feet square and 10 feet high. Opening windows are high in the back, and shallow windows are at the sides above the lining. A building this size provides room for

Fig. 7-4. Make a strongly built barn of traditional shape with double doors and windows at the side.

Front

2 corner posts	2	× 3	×	74
2 door posts	2	× 3	×	86
1 bottom rail	2	× 3	×	134
1 door rail	2	× 3	×	120
4 side rails	2	× 3	×	26
2 uprights	2	× 3	×	26
1 upright	2	× 3	×	36
2 rafters	2	× 3	×	84
2 rafters	2	× 3	×	60

Back

2 corner posts	2	× 3	×	74
2 posts	2	× 3	×	100
1 upright	2	× 3	×	36
3 rails	2	× 3	×	134
1 rail	2	× 3	×	12
1 rail	2	× 3	×	54
2 rafters	2	× 3	×	84
2 rafters	2	× 3	×	60
8 window linings	1	× 4	×	26

Sides

14 uprights	2	× 3	×	74
8 rails	2	× 3	×	130
8 window linings	1	× 4	×	24
16 window linings	1	× 4	×	18
8 window sills	1 1/4	× 5	×	24
4 corner fillers	1	× 2 1/2	×	74

Roof truss

2 rafters	2	× 3	×	60
1 tie	2	× 3	×	48
2 struts	2	× 3	×	120
3 gussets	2	× 3	×	60
	2	× 3	×	36

Roof

1 ridge	2	× 4	×	150
8 purlins	2	× 3	×	150
4 bargeboards	1	× 6	×	90
4 bargeboards	1	× 6	×	80
14 battens	1/2	× 1 1/2	×	84
14 battens	1/2	× 1 1/2	×	60

Doors

7 ledgers	1	× 6	×	42
4 braces	1	× 6	×	70
Covering boards	1-×-6 tongued-and-grooved boards			
3 door linings	1	× 5	×	86
8 edges	1	× 3	×	40

Cladding

ends and sides	1-×-6 shiplap boards or equivalent
roof	1-×-6 plain or tongued-and-grooved boards
doors	1-×-6 plain or tongued-and-grooved boards
lining	1/2 or 3/4 particleboard or plywood

a horse to be stabled, with space for tack and feed. If you are concerned with smaller animals, you can accommodate two or more. The barn would also make a good place to store all the many things you would use on a small farm. The building has an attractive appearance, and you might wish to use it for many purposes in your yard. With different window arrangements, it would make a good workshop. You can alter doors to suit your needs. As shown, the doors are big enough for small trailers or other wheeled vehicles. A motorcycle, trail bike, or even a small car could fit through them.

The drawings and instructions are for a barn framed with 2-inch-×-3-inch-section wood covered with horizontal shiplap boards (FIG. 7-5). Suggested lining material is particleboard or plywood. Measure your available space. Allow for laying a concrete base larger than the barn area. You must securely bolt down a building this size. You may prefabricate the ends and sides. Roofing is done in position after you have erected the walls.

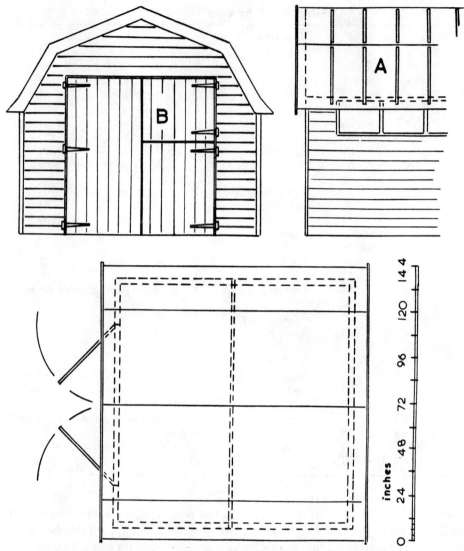

Fig. 7-5. Suggested sizes for the barn.

Start by making the ends (FIG. 7-6). The back (FIG. 7-6A) is closed, but the front has a 7-foot-square doorway (FIG. 7-6B). Assemble framing with the 3-inch way towards the cladding. Halve or tenon joints in the framing. Halve crossing parts of internal framing. The central rail is at the height intended for the lining. If that height does not suit your needs, alter its position. This height allows for shallow windows above the lining and under the eaves. Angles for the roof are shown (FIG. 7-6C). If you do not work exactly to these angles, it does not matter, as long as each end is symmetrical and they match.

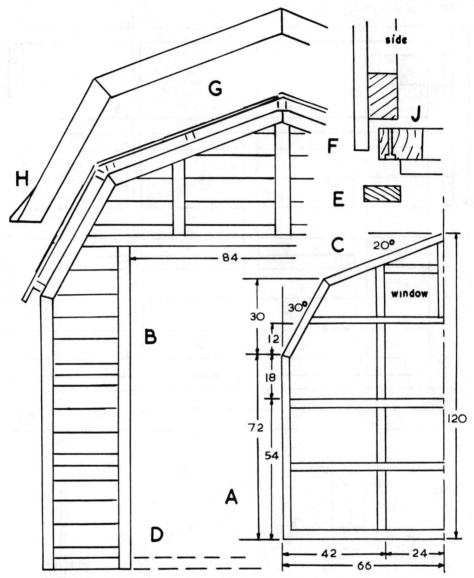

Fig. 7-6. *Details of the ends of the barn, which you should make first.*

Make the back and use it as a pattern for the outline of the front. Make the bottom rail of the front right across (FIG. 7-6D), but after you have erected the walls and anchored them down, you can cut it away to give a clear door opening. You can improve appearance of the ends if you add a broad filler piece at each corner (FIG. 7-6E). To allow for this filler piece, stop the shiplap boards over the center of the corner posts. Take them to the edges of the roof slopes.

The two sides are the same (FIG. 7-7A), unless you want to fit a side door or

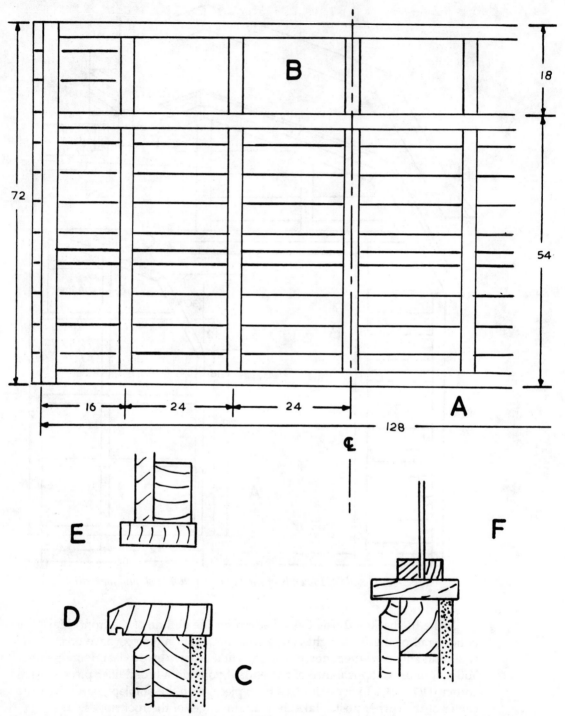

Fig. 7-7. A side of the barn and sections at the windows.

alter the number of windows. The drawing shows four window openings on each side (FIG. 7-7B), but you could reduce this to two or none. The tops of the windows are covered by the roof, so you cannot arrange them to swing outwards very much. They could open inwards, but it probably will be satisfactory to make them fixed.

Allow for the cladding boards extending at the ends to cover the end corner posts (FIG. 7-6F). Finish level at top and bottom. You do not have to bevel the top to match the slope of the roof.

You could add the lining at this stage or leave it until after erection. Take it to the window line (FIG. 7-7C). Cover it there with a sill extending outwards (FIG. 7-7D). Line the tops and sides of the openings (FIG. 7-7E). The roof will provide protection to the upper parts of the windows.

The roof needs a truss halfway along. This truss must match the ends of the building, so use one of the ends as a pattern for the shape. The outline is the same down to the top of the side panels. As no boards are across to strengthen the framing, securely nail or screw gussets under the angles (FIG. 7-8A). The tie is the same height as the rail above the doorway. From its center, take struts at 45 degrees to it, up to the rafters (FIG. 7-8B). Cut the rafters to rest on the tops of the side frames, with locating blocks there (FIG. 7-8C). The purlins are 2 inches × 3 inches, and the ridge is from 2-inch-×-4-inch stock. Bevel the top of the ridge piece to match the slope of the roof (FIG. 7-8D). These slopes have to match the tops of the purlins. Measure their heights, and cut down the tops of the ends and the truss so the roof at the ridge will be the same height from the framing as it is at the purlins (FIG. 7-8E).

Make cleats to position and hold the ridge and purlins (FIG. 7-8F). At the angle of the roof, put the purlins as close together as possible. The top purlins

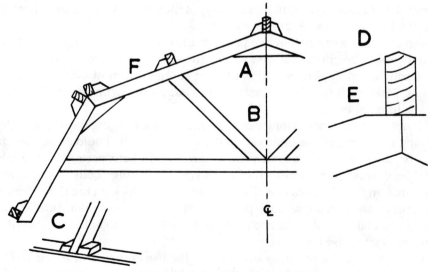

Fig. 7-8. Details of the barn-roof truss.

are midway between the angle of the roof and the ridge. The lower purlins should come close to the joint with the sides.

Assemble the walls, using 1/2-inch bolts. Sink their heads so the cover strips will hide them (FIG. 7-6J). For ample strength in any circumstances, have the bolts at about 12-inch centers. Check squareness and fasten down to the base. Cut out the bottom of the end frame under the doorway. If necessary, nail on temporary braces to keep the building square and to hold the truss upright until you fit the roof.

The purlins and ridge should extend 6 inches at each end. Fix them in position. The roof covering could be shingles over 1/2-inch plywood, but 1-inch boarding, covered by roofing felt or any of the sheet-roof material supplied in a roll, taken over the ridge and turned under the roof boards as described for several other buildings, is suggested. Cut the board ends to meet reasonably close at the ridge and at the angles. Take the ends of the boards to about 1 inch below the tops of the building sides. A gap will be all around under the roof boards. You can leave the gap entirely or in part for ventilation, or you can fill the narrow spaces against the lower purlins or the wider gaps between purlins at the ends.

Make bargeboards at the end (FIG. 7-6G). Take the ends a short distance below the roof edges. You can give a traditional appearance with triangles if you turn the board line outwards (FIG. 7-6H). Put battens down the slope of the roof over the covering at about 18-inch intervals (FIG. 7-5A).

The double doors are ledgered and braced, but because of their size and weight, you must double them around the edges (FIG. 7-9A). Put lining strips around the door opening, covering the wall lining as well as the cladding (FIG. 7-9B). Make the doors with vertical tongue-and-groove boards. Put braces across, level with the board ends, and fill in to the same thickness at the edges (FIG. 7-9C). So the diagonal braces take any compression loads that come on them without allowing movement, fit them closely at their ends, making sure there are no gaps which might cause the door to drop.

You could make one half in two parts for the usual stable door pattern (FIGS. 7-5B and 7-9D). A height of 48 inches would give a horse about 36 inches to put its head through, but the gap would not be big enough for most animals to jump through. Make each door part similar to the large door, with bracing upwards from the hinge side.

T hinges about 18 inches long would be suitable for hanging the doors. Notch the lining strips around the doorway for the hinges, which should come over the ledges on the doors and be held with long screws in both parts. You can take bolts right through to nuts instead of using screws. Arrange bolts upwards and downwards on the inner edge of one door, and place a lock on the other door to close it or a hasp and staple for a padlock. Put handles on the outside of both doors. If you make one door in two parts, put a bolt inside to hold them together when you want to use the parts as one.

How you make the windows depends on the use of the barn. If you want it to be weathertight, the windows should be made closely. The overhang of the

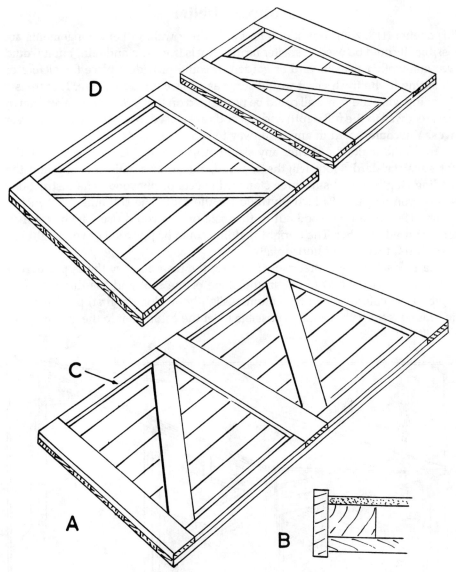

Fig. 7-9. Construction of the barn doors.

roof, however, gives partial protection to the windows, and you can use a simple construction if a slight risk of leakage is not important. With the window openings lined, you can hold glass in between double strips (FIG. 7-7F). You could embed the glass in jointing compound, but another way would be to put single strips around the glass and putty the glass against them.

For better windows, frame them separately to fit in the openings (FIG. 5-4). If you want any windows to open by being hinged at the top, make them this way.

Animal Shelter

This shelter (FIG. 7-10) consist of a roof and a rear wall. Other arrangements are possible. It could be used to shelter farm animals from sun and rain, but it would have many other uses in yard or garden. It could provide a place for picnics or just sitting in the fresh air. It would serve as a place for a barbecue. If there is a prevailing wind the rear wall could be positioned on that side. The shelter shown has a rear wall to the full depth and the ends are closed in as far down as the rear eaves. You could board in any other way to suit your needs.

You could make the shelter any size, but as drawn (FIGS. 7-11 and 7-12), the roof suits standard 8-foot lengths of wood, metal, or plastic covering and the building length would suit three standard sheets of plywood. The instructions assume you will use 3/4-inch plywood for the roof. The columns are 4 inches square. They could be wood cut to that size or you could use 2-inch-×-4-inch stock screwed together. The upright cladding could be plywood or you might use strips of solid wood laid horizontally.

Start by setting out, preferably full-size, the main lines of the upper part of an end view (FIG. 7-11A) to obtain the slope of the roof and the differences in length of the columns. Cut the columns slightly overlong at first, particularly if the ground is very uneven. It is possible to let the columns into the ground with concrete.

Fig. 7-10. *This simple shelter provides protection from wind and rain for animals.*

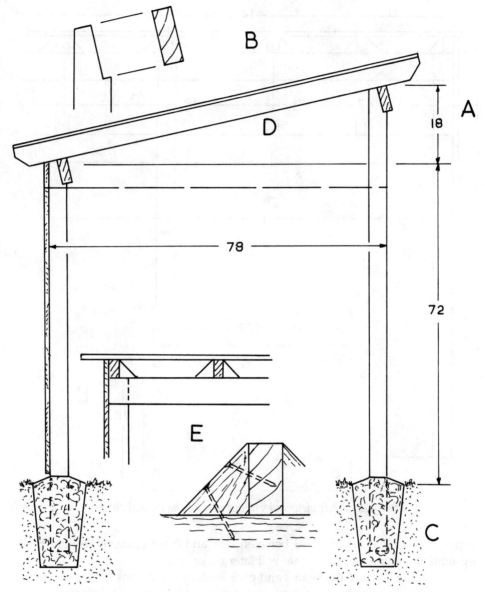

Fig. 7-11. End view of the animal shelter.

Bevel the tops of the columns and notch them to take the beams (FIG. 7-11B). Cut the beams to length and mark on them the positions of the intermediate columns and the rafters (FIG. 7-12A). Note that two rafters come under plywood roof joints.

Set out the positions of the columns on the ground (FIG. 7-12B) and dig the holes. Put the columns in the holes and clamp the beams to their tops. Clamp or

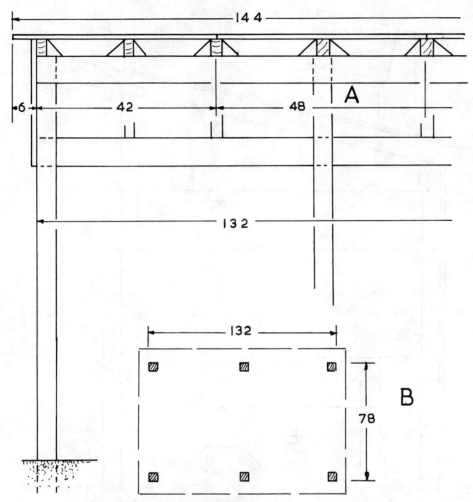

Fig. 7-12. Front view and ground plan of the animal shelter.

temporarily nail strips of wood between rear and front columns to hold them upright. You could use wood that will later make rafters.

Check the levels of the beams and pack under the columns where necessary. See that the assembly is upright and square. Concrete the bottoms of the columns (FIG. 7-11C).

When the concrete has set, nail the beams to the columns. Prepare the seven rafters (FIG. 7-11D). Bevel the ends for neatness. Attach them to the beams with triangular brackets (FIG. 7-11E). Cut these with their grain diagonally.

Nail the sheets for the plywood roof to the rafters, starting with the meeting edges over rafters. Cover with felt or similar material. You could put strips of about 3/4-inch-×-1 1/2-inch wood under the outer edges for stiffness and more security for nails through the felt.

Materials List for Animal Shelter

3 columns	4	× 4	×	108
3 columns	4	× 4	×	96
2 beams	2	× 6	×	134
7 rafters	2	× 4	×	98
3 roof sheets	48	× 96	×	3/4 plywood
Cladding	1	× 6 or 3/4 plywood		
20 brackets from	2	× 4	×	108 or offcuts

Cover the rear wall with plywood or use strips of about 1-inch-×-6-inch section across. Cover the ends from under the roof down to the rear eaves line in a similar way. Finish with preservative or paint.

8

Children's Buildings

Children at play like to have something to get into. With a house of their own, they can spend many happy hours of make-believe.

Children grow up, so anything you make should be big enough to last a child a few years. If you think you might want to eventually take such a structure apart, you could arrange joints that would let you salvage at least some of the materials. If you do not have space for a permanent small building, this chapter shows you how to make a building to fold or take apart.

Remember always the need for safety. Avoid splintery wood, and round all corners and edges. If you want more than a hole for a window, cover it with soft transparent plastic, not glass.

Basic Folding Playhouse

You can make the simplest small playhouse entirely from 1/2-inch plywood panels, hinging them together so it is portable. The house shown in FIG. 8-1 has a roof that lifts off and ends that are hinged centrally (FIG. 8-2A) so it is possible to fold the parts into a bundle under 5 inches thick. The greatest packed length is 48 inches, and the greatest packed width is 38 inches. Sizes are arranged so you can cut them economically from 48-inch-×-96-inch plywood sheets (FIG. 8-2B). As shown, there are openings for a window and a door. You could hinge on a plywood door and fit plastic sheet to the window, although for the age child this is intended for, simple openings should be satisfying.

Be careful to square all parts, or they will not fit and fold properly. Make four end pieces (FIG. 8-3A). With these sizes, the roof will slope at about 30 degrees.

Fig. 8-1. *You can make a basic folding playhouse from plywood sheets.*

Materials List for Basic Folding Playhouse

4 ends	18- x -48- x -½ plywood
1 front	38- x -45- x -½ plywood
1 back	38- x -45- x -½ plywood
2 roofs	24- x -48- x -½ plywood
4 roof strips	1 x 1 x 21

Make the back and front to match each other and as high as the eaves on the ends (FIG. 8-3B). Cut the door and window openings in the front. Remove sharpness from all edges and round the door and window edges thoroughly.

It should be sufficient to put three 2-inch hinges on each joint. So the parts will fold against each other, the hinges at the centers of the ends come outside (FIG. 8-2C), and those between the ends and the back and front are inside (FIG. 8-2D).

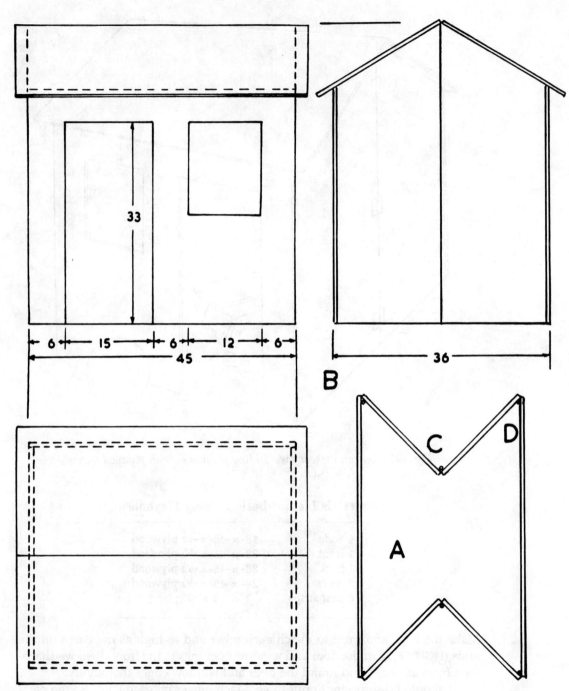

Fig. 8-2. Sizes of the playhouse and the method of folding the walls.

Screws probably will not hold adequately in ½-inch plywood. Although it might be possible to use small nuts and bolts, the neatest way of fixing the hinges is by riveting. The riveting avoids projections that could scratch young hands. You can make suitable rivets with soft-metal nails: copper is particularly suitable. Drill slightly undersize for each nail, and drive it through from the other side. Cut off the nail end to leave sufficient length to hammer into the countersunk hole in the hinge (FIG. 8-3C). Support the nail head on an iron block, and work around the projecting end so as to spread it gradually, preferably using a

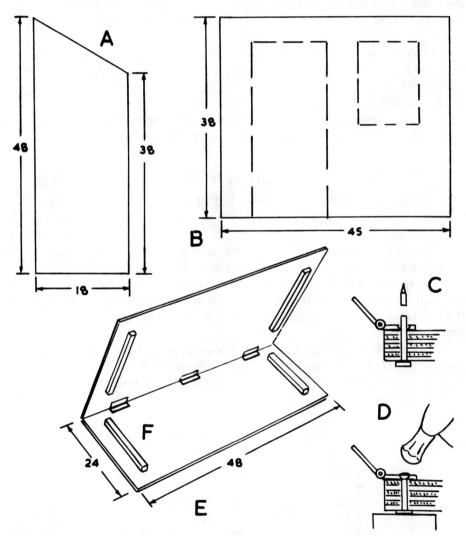

Fig. 8-3. Sizes of the folding playhouse parts and the method of riveting the hinges.

light ball-peen hammer. Try to fill the countersink (FIG. 8-3D). Any excess may be filed off. Adjust the amount the hinge knuckle projects so the ends will open flat and the corners finish close when square to each other.

The two roof sections (FIG. 8-3E) will overlap the walls by a small amount. Hinge them together and locate them on the assembled walls so the overhangs are even. Mark the positions of the ends under the roof. Glue and nail strips to fit inside the ends (FIG. 8-3F). Their lower ends should come against the front and back, but the upper ends may be cut back about 2 inches. The roof then will hold the walls in shape. This procedure might be all you need to do, but if the child is able to push the roof, you could fit hooks and eyes outside, under the roof at the ends.

Finish the house in bright colors, with the outside walls a different color from the roof and the inside walls a lighter color. You could edge the openings with a darker color.

If you fit a door, it may be a piece of plywood hinged outside. Put a strip across a top corner inside to act as a stop. A wooden turnbutton outside will allow the child to "lock" the door when leaving the house.

General Store

Children like to play at shopkeeping. The little building shown in FIG. 8-4 is intended to give them a store into which they can put the things they want to pretend to sell. A counter in the window lets them serve customers, and they can close a door to stop anyone unauthorized from getting inside. There could be a back door if they have so much stock that some has to go outside.

Construction is with 1/2-inch plywood and some 1-inch-×-2-inch strip framing. Bolt parts together so the structure is semipermanent, but so you can fold flat sheets for storage. It is not intended to be very weathertight, but the parts would not suffer if rained on occasionally.

The sizes shown should suit most children of an age likely to use the building, but you might wish to modify them to suit your children or available space. You can cut the parts without much waste from standard 48-inch-×-96-inch sheets (FIG. 8-5A).

Materials List for General Store

1 front	48- × -72- × -½ plywood
1 back	45- × -66- × -½ plywood
2 sides	36- × -39- × -½ plywood
2 roofs	36- × -39- × -½ plywood
1 door	18- × -36- × -½ plywood
1 counter	12- × -30- × -½ plywood
2 counter strips	1 × 2 × 30
8 framing strips	1 × 2 × 39

Fig. 8-4. A child can use this general store to pretend to sell goods.

Make the back first. The roof has a shallow slope to give maximum head room at the sides. Put 1-inch-×-2-inch strips around the edges, level with the roof slopes, but in from the sides by the thickness of the side plywood (FIGS. 8-5B and 8-6A). Fit the sides in and bolt through them. Glue and screws are advisable to attach the framing to the end plywood.

Cut the front to size and use the back as a pattern to lay out a matching arrangement of strips (FIG. 8-6B). Also mark the positions of the door and window (FIG. 8-5C). It will be easier to cut these parts before you attach the strips. Take sharpness off the edges and round the upper parts of the window opening. Cut a door opening in the back, if you wish.

The two sides are plain rectangles (FIG. 8-5D). At each corner, drill for three 1/4-inch coach bolts. You can make a window opening in one or both sides, but it probably will be better if you leave them solid. In this size building, there should be no need to fasten the roof to the sides, but if you make the store longer from front to back, place a strip matching the slope of the roof along each top edge to take bolts through the roof.

Assemble the parts made so far so you can test the fit of the roof panels as you make them. Place them against the front, over the strips there. At the back, they can project about 1 inch and at the sides they should project almost to the width of the front (FIG. 8-6C). Hinge the panels together along the ridge, prefera-

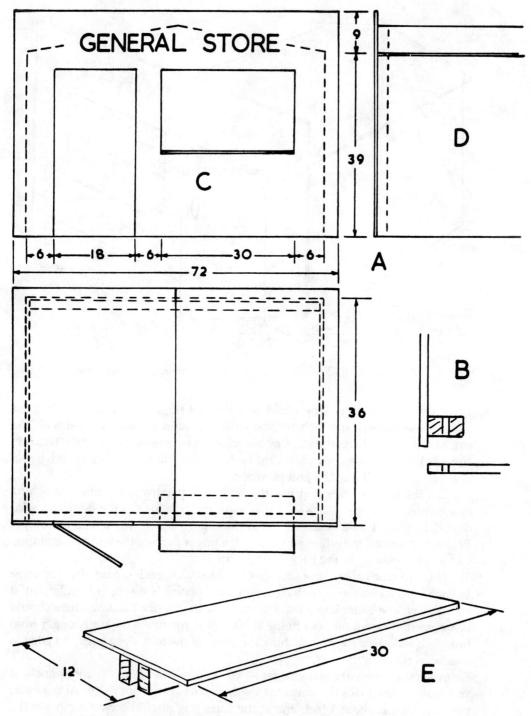

GENERAL STORE

C

D

A

6 18 6 30 6

72

B

36

9

39

12

30

E

Fig. 8-5. Sizes of parts of the child's general store.

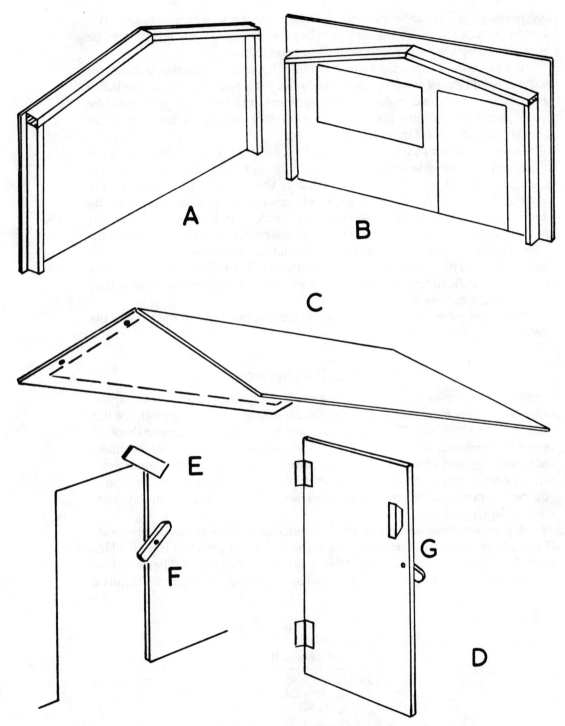

Fig. 8-6. Construction of the parts of the child's store.

bly riveting the hinges in the way described for the folding playhouse (FIG. 8-3C,D). At back and front, drill for two bolts on each slope. These bolts should be enough to keep the roof on and hold the assembly in shape.

You can make the serving counter set into the window opening permanent, but that would interfere with packing the house flat if you disassemble the building. Instead, you could make it with two strips underneath to press over the lower part of the window (FIG. 8-5E). This assembly should be firm enough in use, but you can lift off the counter.

Make a door from a piece of plywood (FIG. 8-6D). Allow easy clearance at the sides, and you can make the bottom up to 1 inch from the ground. A strip inside the top corner will act as a stop and be out of the way (FIG. 8-6E). Rivet on the hinges, although if you want to screw, place a thin strip of wood behind the doorway to take their points. There could be wooden turnbuttons inside and out so the shopkeeper can shut out intruders or fasten the door when he leaves his store. The outside turnbutton must be on the side of the doorway (FIG. 8-6F). The inside one must be on the edge of the door (FIG. 8-6G). The inside turnbutton will serve as a handle inside, but you should add a block of wood or some sort of handle on the outside of the door.

When you paint in bright colors, you could put the name of the store or the child's own name on the front.

Pack-Flat Playhouse

If you want to provide a playhouse for a small child and do not have the space indoors or outdoors to store a complete little building, this project might be the answer for you (FIG. 8-7). The assembled house has an inside floor area about 28 inches by 44 inches, and the total height is 48 inches. You could alter the sizes, but those suggested allow for economical cutting from standard plywood sheets. When taken apart you have seven pieces of plywood without projections, so if you use 1/2-inch plywood, the packed thickness is 3 1/2 inches, or you can separate into lesser packages.

All parts are plywood. You could use 1/2-inch fir or other softwood plywood. Hardwood plywood need only be 3/8 inch thick. Exterior plywood is preferable, but if the playhouse is unlikely to get wet, any other plywood could be used. Cut edges carefully, both to ensure good fits and to avoid roughness that might hurt a

Materials List for
Pack-Flat Playhouse
(all 1/2-inch plywood)

2 ends	32	× 48
2 sides	32	× 48
2 roofs	28	× 48
1 shelf	9	× 32

Fig. 8-7. The parts of this playhouse hook together and can be disassembled to pack flat.

child. Softwood plywood, in particular, should be cleaned free of splintery or rough edges, by thorough sanding.

For the sizes suggested (FIG. 8-8A), all of the parts can be cut alongside each other across standard 4-foot-×-8-foot sheets, as the walls and roof are all 48 inches long and the shelf a little shorter.

The four walls hook together (FIG. 8-9A). There is a shelf inside (FIG. 8-8B). For the smallest child this could be a table, but a bigger child will treat it as a seat. Its purpose structurally is to ensure squareness of the assembly, aided by the roof sections, which fit onto lugs in the ends (FIG. 8-9B).

Before marking out the walls, examine details of the hooks and sockets (FIG. 8-10). The sockets in the end walls are 4 inches long and wide enough to fit easily over the thickness of the plywood (FIG. 8-10A)—$5/8$ inch would be suitable

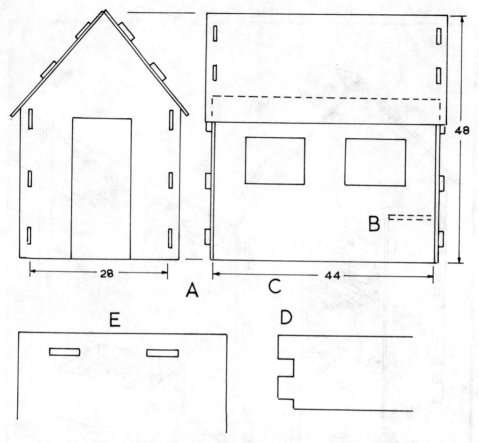

Fig. 8-8. Suggested sizes for the pack-flat playhouse. Roof and shelf details.

for 1/2-inch plywood. The hooks (FIG. 8-10B) are passed through the sockets, then moved down to fasten over the lower edges of the sockets, while bottom edges of the walls are brought level with each other. It is important in marking out that spacings all match (FIG. 8-9C). If possible, make corner joints interchangeable. If they do not match each other closely enough, mark the corners which should be fitted to each other.

Mark out and cut the two ends (FIG. 8-9D) with identical outlines, but only one with a doorway. The lugs on the roof slopes are 4 inches long and 3 inches from the corners. They should project 1 1/2 inches, with rounded corners.

Make the two side walls (FIGS. 8-8C and 8-9E), with windows in one or both pieces. The key markings for the hooks are the positions of the bottom edges of the sockets on the end walls, so lower edges of walls will assemble level. Work from these points to mark and cut the hook outlines. Check that the top of the side walls come level with the slopes of the end pieces.

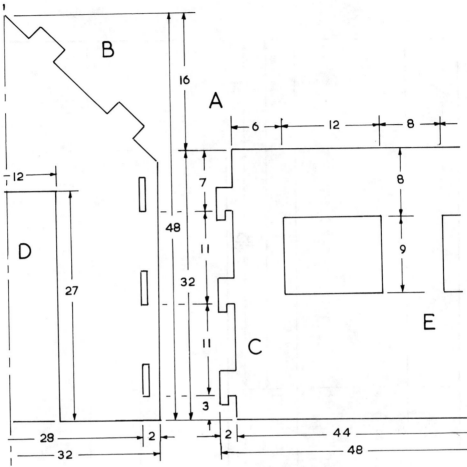

Fig. 8-9. Sizes of side and end of the pack-flat playhouse.

While you test assemble the four walls, measure inside for the length of the shelf. Make it 9 inches wide, with lugs (FIG. 8-8D) to pass through sockets in the walls. Arrange the shelf to fit closely against the rear wall to hold the assembly square.

Make the roof sections 48 inches long and wide enough to overhang a little at the eaves. If you have worked to the sizes suggested, this will be 28 inches. Using a trial assembly of the walls and shelf, mark the positions of sockets (FIG. 8-8E). Round exposed edges and corners.

This completes the making of parts. Take off any roughness at edges before painting. You could just paint the walls one color and the roof another, but you might prefer to decorate by drawing on framing around door and windows and possibly marking lines to indicate siding. Inside there could be lighter paint, or

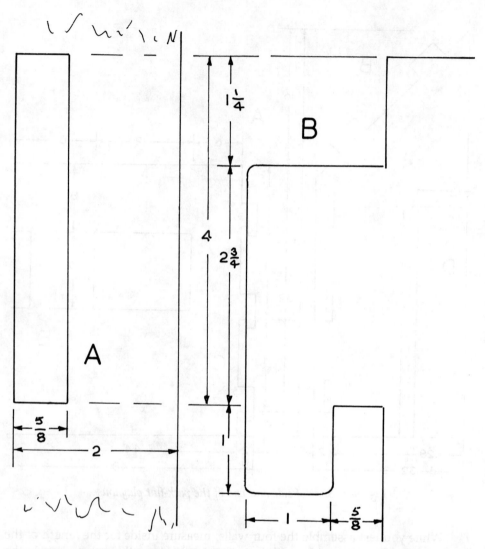

Fig. 8-10. Sizes of the hooks and slots used for assembly of the playhouse.

you could stick on wallpaper. If thickness is to be kept minimal, you cannot add anything that projects, but you might glue on cloth to hang inside the windows.

Tree House

The idea of a house in a tree appeals to young people. It is romantic, and there is a sense of adventure. Each tree house has to be an individual design because it depends on the tree, so no materials list is provided for this project. In general you have to choose a tree that is strong enough, has a suitable arrangement of branches, and that will make a house of a suitable size at a convenient height. For peace of mind of parents, the height might only be 7 feet to the platform, but you have to arrange the layout to make best use of parts of the tree.

The tree should have a rigid trunk and sufficient branches that are strong enough to allow attachments. Driving nails into the tree or cutting off some branches should not affect the life of the tree. You can cut shallow notches into

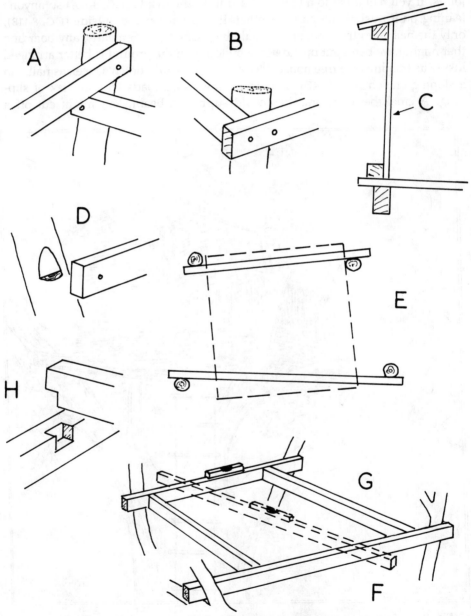

Fig. 8-11. Suggested construction of the tree house.

branches. You must avoid cutting away so much that there is little bark left: Much of the tree's lifeblood is in the sap that goes up and down under the bark.

Any tree house is basically a platform on which there could be a roofed shelter and an open area fenced around. There has to be space for access via a ladder, but except for that opening you must prevent the users' falling off.

For security, arrange the structures so outward-thrusting loads cannot break joints. If you nail a rail to a branch, have it on the inside (FIG. 8-11A) so anyone leaning on it pushes the parts together. If you nail on the outside (FIG. 8-11B), only the nail takes the load, and it could be pushed out. Similarly, any boarding that might have been put outside on a building on the ground is better arranged inside its framing on a tree house (FIG. 8-11C). You could notch as well as nail into a sloping branch (FIG. 8-11D). This takes downward loads without risk of slipping. A crook between branches could support a beam. You might cut off a

Fig. 8-12. In this example, it is assumed you can arrange a platform 7 feet square.

branch so it comes under and supports the house, or you might prefer to let it pass through the platform.

The platform has to be mounted level (FIG. 8-11E). Relating that need to the form of the tree might determine the final height. Experiment with two strips of wood across what will be attachment points. You have to get two beams across, both at the same level and as near as possible to the width of the intended platform. You can expect to have to modify your ideas to suit supporting branches. It is unlikely the beams can be parallel, and they might not be as far apart as the size you want the platform.

If the platform is to be about 7 feet square, the beams could be at least a 2-inch- × -4-inch section. Get one beam level, probably fitted into notches and temporarily clamped or tied on. Locate the other one by sighting across to see that it is level and by checking the level across with strips (FIG. 8-11F). You might be able to arrange more than two beams at this level, depending on available parts of the tree to provide support. In any case, put other beams between the first two, with their tops level (FIG. 8-11G). Notched joints at the ends (FIG. 8-11H) can supplement nails. This pattern of beams provides the strength members. Make sure the beams are secure and will form a sound level base for anything you put on top.

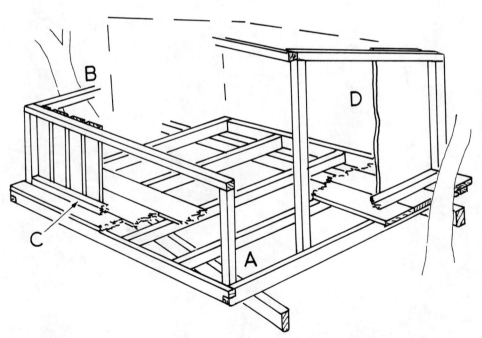

Fig. 8-13. *Nail or bolt the uprights (A), and top the posts with rails (B). Fit strips along to take the palings (C) after you have put down the floorboards. Use boards or plywood inside for framing (D).*

The size and shape of the platform will depend on available space. Corners do not have to be square but are better that way. For the example, we assume you can arrange a platform 7 feet square (FIG. 8-12). This can project outside the supporting beams and possibly go around a branch. Use 2-inch-×-4-inch wood covered with 1-inch boards. Notch frame parts together. Attach them to the beams, and lay out uprights before putting down the floor boards. Nail or bolt the uprights into angles between frame parts (FIG. 8-13A). For the open parts, top the posts with rails (FIG. 8-13B). After you have put down the floor boards, fit strips along to take the upright palings inside (FIG. 8-13C). The palings could be 1-inch-×-4-inch pieces with 1-inch gaps.

For the covered part, take posts to the heights needed. Frame in a similar way to the other buildings, except use boards or plywood inside (FIG. 8-13D). Children will probably be satisfied with less than full-standing head room. A plywood roof should be satisfactory. As you arrange posts, rails, and building framing, consider any further support the tree could provide. You might be able to extend a part to attach to another branch. Any additional support is worth having.

Access could be with an ordinary ladder leant in place and taken away when the house is not in use. There could be a rope ladder supported through holes in a beam.

Glossary

The making of wooden buildings is only part of the much wider craft of woodworking. The selection of words that follows includes some that are particularly appropriate to the subject of this book and might be helpful to readers unfamiliar with the language of this branch of the craft.

ark   A building for small animals.
aviary   A building to hold birds.

bargeboards   Covering boards at the gable end of a roof.
battens   Strips of wood of light section, used on a roof to hold down the covering.
brace   A diagonal strut used to triangulate an assembly and prevent it distorting.

chipboard   A board made by bonding wood chips with a synthetic resin. Also called *particleboard*.
cladding   The covering of boards that forms the outside of a wall.
cleat   A link between other parts. A strip of wood across other pieces. A support for a purlin on a rafter.
coach bolt   Alternative name for carriage bolt. A bolt for use with a nut, having a shallow round head and a square neck to grip the wood.
coach screw   Alternative name for a wood screw, with a square head for use with a wrench. Also called a *lag screw*.
corrugated sheet   Roofing material, which might be steel, other metal, or plastic. Corrugations in the length provide stiffness.
cut nail   A nail made from sheet steel instead of the more usual wire.

drip groove A groove cut along the underside of a sill or other projecting wood to prevent water running back.

eaves The angle between the roof and a wall. The overhang of a roof over a wall. Never spelled without the *s*, even if there is only one.

exterior-grade plywood Plywood in which the glue used is waterproof.

eye screw Alternative name for screw eye. A screw for wood with a ring or eye as head.

fascia A long flat wooden surface, such as the front of a lean-to roof.

gable The end of a roof, usually one with a ridge.

galvanizing A method of coating steel with zinc as a protection against rust. Used on corrugated steel roof sheets.

gambrel roof Alternative name for *mansard roof*. A roof with two slopes on each side.

gazebo A structure intended to be decorative and, usually, from which you can obtain a view.

hardboard A thin board made from compressed shredded wood.

hardwood Wood from broad-leafed trees, which shed their leaves in the winter.

hip roof The end of a ridge roof that slopes inwards instead of having a vertical gable.

joist A supporting beam, as in a floor.

lag screw Alternative name for a coach screw.

lean-to A building with a roof having a single slope. It could be against another building or be free-standing.

ledger, ledged A piece across the vertical boards of a door, used with braces to keep the door in shape.

lintel Support for a load over a doorway or other opening.

mansard roof Alternative name for a gambrel roof.

nominal When applied to lumber, this is the sawn size, and wood finished by machine planing will have smaller sections.

palisade, or paling A fence of upright boards.

particleboard Alternative name for chipboard.

pergola A wooden structure covered with growing plants.

pitch Slope of a roof. Distance between tops of a screw thread.

plywood Manufactured board made by gluing thin pieces of wood (veneers or plies) with the grain of alternate pieces arranged at right angles.

pole construction A barn or other building made with poles as the main structural parts.

pop hole The entrance for poultry into their house.

purlin A lengthwise support for roof covering, usually supported on rafters.

rabbet (rebate) Recess in the edge of wood, as in a picture frame.

rafter A support for a roof.

rail A horizontal structural member.

ridge The apex of a roof made like an inverted V.

roofing felt A flexible roof covering material to lay over boards or plywood, made of felt impregnated with tar, asphalt or other waterproof substance.

roof truss A braced framework with rafters for supporting a roof.

screw eye Alternative name for eye screw.

shiplap boards Cladding boards, to be laid horizontally, with the upper edge of each one fitting into a rabbet in the one above.

sill (cill) A projecting horizontal board, such as the bottom of a window, to shed water away from the wall below.

softwood Wood from needle-leaf trees.

stable door A door in two parts, so you can open the top part while the lower part remains closed.

staple A nail in the form of a U, so it has double points.

stressed skin An assembly in which the skin plays a major part in providing strength.

sway bracing Diagonal pieces to triangulate an assembly and provide a resistance to distortion, particularly in strong winds.

tack A small tapered nail. Harness and other equipment used with a horse.

tempered hardboard Hardboard treated with oil, to strengthen it and give it a resistance to water.

tie A member under tension in a structure, as across a roof truss, where it prevents rafters spreading.

tongue-and-groove boards Boards prepared so a tongue on the edge of one piece fits the groove on the edge of the next piece.

triangulation Placing a member diagonally across a four-sided figure to divide it into triangles, so it keeps its shape.

truss A supporting structural framework. In a building, rafters might be supported by truss.

waney edge   The shape of the outside of a tree retained on the edge of a board that has not been squared.

weatherboarding   Cladding boards to be laid horizontally, tapered in the width so the thin edge of a lower board goes under the thicker lower edge of the one above it.

wind bracing   Sway bracing arranged in the roof, diagonally between trusses or purlins, to resist distorting loads in the roof due to strong winds.

Index

Other Bestsellers of Related Interest

CREATIVE GARDEN SETTINGS
—John D. Webersinn and G. Daniel Keen

Look at the ways you can landscape your property and turn your house into a panorama of outdoor creativity, at the same time increasing the value of your home. Whether you want to build a deck, a patio, a stone fence, or a trickling fountain—nothing is beyond your reach. Keen and Webersinn combine their skills to bring you a well-written guide to everything from building permits to outdoor lighting. 200 pages, 100 illustrations. Book No. 3936, $14.95 paperback, $24.95 hardcover

TROUBLESHOOTING AND REPAIRING SOLID-STATE TVs—2nd Edition
—Homer L. Davidson

With this updated, complete workbench reference, you will have practical information on troubleshooting and repairing all the most recent solid-state TV circuitry used by the major manufacturers of all brands and models of TVs. This new edition includes the latest material on high-definition TV, or HDTV, and spike bar protectors, as well as in-depth looks at particular circuits from Sylvania, RCA, Radio Shack, and Panasonic televisions. 624 pages, 698 illustrations. Book No. 3700, $24.95 paperback, $36.95 hardcover

GARDENING FOR A GREENER PLANET: A Chemical-Free Approach—Jonathan Erickson

Control pests in your lawn and garden with these environmentally safe methods. Using a technique known as "integrated pest management," this book shows you how to protect food and foliage from destructive insects without contamination from toxins found in chemical pesticides. He explains, in easy-to-follow steps, the correct way to use natural methods such as beneficial insects and organisms, companion planting, minerals and soaps, and botanical insecticides in the war against garden-hungry bugs. 176 pages, 108 illustrations. 8-page full-color insert. Book No. 3801, $13.95 paperback, $21.95 hardcover

BRICKLAYING: A Homeowner's Illustrated Guide—Charles R. Self

In this handy do-it-yourself guide you'll learn the basics of bricklaying: how to create different pattern bonds, mix mortar, lay bricks to achieve the strongest structure, cut bricks, finish mortar joints, and estimate materials. You'll also find out how to mix, test, and pour concrete to create foundations and footings for your brickwork. With the step-by-step instructions and illustrations found here, you can build any project with little difficulty. 176 pages, 146 illustrations. Book No. 3878, $14.95 paperback, $22.95 hardcover

DECKS AND PATIOS: Designing and Building Outdoor Living Spaces—Edward A. Baldwin

This handsome book will show you step by step how to take advantage of outdoor space. It's a comprehensive guide to designing and building decks and patios that fit the style of your home and the space available. You'll find coverage of a variety of decks, patios, walkways, and stairs. Baldwin helps you design your outdoor project, and then shows you how to accomplish every step from site preparation through finishing and preserving your work to ensure many years of enjoyment. 152 pages, 180 illustrations. Book No. 3326, $16.95 paperback, $26.95 hardcover

FENCES, DECKS AND OTHER BACKYARD PROJECTS—2nd Edition—Dan Ramsey

Do-it-yourself—design, build, and landscape fences and other outdoor structures. This is the most complete guide available for choosing, installing, and properly maintaining every kind of fence. Plus, there are how-to's for a variety of outdoor structures, from sheds and decks to greenhouses and gazebos. You get easy-to-follow instructions, work-in-progress diagrams, tables, and hundreds of illustrations. 304 pages, illustrated. Book No. 2778, $15.95 paperback only

GIFTS FROM THE WOODSHOP
—R. J. De Cristoforo

Whether you're a master craftsman or novice woodbutcher, you'll find something challenging in this collection of practical and attractive gift projects. You'll find instructions for building kitchen aids, plant hangers and stands, wind chimes, bird houses and feeders, toys, picture and mirror frames, shelves and racks, decorative plaques, and much more. All projects can be made using basic hand tools. 240 pages, 290 illustrations. Book No. 3591, $15.95 paperback, $24.95 hardcover

ALTERNATIVE ENERGY PROJECTS FOR THE 1990s—John A. Kuecken

Free yourself from high energy bills by using this newly revised edition of the 50,000-copy seller. It provides clear, illustrated instructions for building instruments that can harness enough wind, water, or sunlight to meet a large percentage of home electricity needs. And it includes computer programs for making calculations, information on small windmills, and the new Power Tower. 264 pages, 140 illustrations. Book No. 3835, $14.95 paperback, $22.95 hardcover

GARDEN TOOLS AND GADGETS YOU CAN MAKE—Percy W. Blandford

This book boasts project plans for just about any garden convenience or accessory you can think of! All of them will make gardening more enjoyable, productive, and easier—you'll be amazed at the money you can save by making your own garden tools. Step-by-step instructions and detailed illustrations accompany each project. Included are small hand tools, boxes, bins, climbing supports, carts, buildings, and more. 260 pages, illustrated. Book No. 3194, $11.95 paperback, $18.95 hardcover

THE DRILL PRESS BOOK: Including 80 Jigs and Accessories to Make—R. J. De Cristoforo

The drill press, after the table saw, is the second most important tool in the workshop. In this well-illustrated guide, you'll discover unique ways to develop the tool's potential in over 80 project plans. As De Cristoforo guides you through each application of this versatile tool, you'll benefit from hundreds of hints based on his years of woodworking experience. 304 pages, 406 illustrations. Book No. 3609, $16.95 paperback, $25.95 hardcover